Prize-wi

CW01073063

50 Tickets to Ri
Heathrow Express

Complete the form below and send it to the IPD by 31 December 1998 to enter our draw for one of 50 free single-journey tickets to ride on Heathrow Express.

IPD Books
Institute of Personnel and Development
IPD House
Camp Road
London SW19 4UX

Please use block capitals

Name _

Job title _

Address _

Town _

Postcode _

Winners will be notified by post. The prize is not transferable. For a full list of prize-winners please write to the above address enclosing a stamped addressed envelope after 15 January 1999.

This competition is not open to Institute of Personnel and Development or Heathrow Express, BAA employees or their families, their representatives or agents.

We may send you details of other products and services offered by the IPD. If you do not wish us to do so please indicate by placing a cross in this box ☐

Issued by IPD Enterprises Ltd, a subsidiary of the Institute of Personnel and Development providing commercial services. The Institute of Personnel and Development is a Registered Charity No. 1038333.

Fast Track to Change

on the

Heathrow Express

Sue Lownds is co-founder of Warren Lownds Limited, the organisational development and training consultancy that developed and implemented the 'people' elements of the Heathrow Express change programme. She is a Fellow of the Institute of Personnel and Development, and has spent 17 years as a professional trainer and HR practitioner in a wide range of sectors and organisations.

The Institute of Personnel and Development is the leading publisher of books and reports for personnel and training professionals and students and for all those concerned with the effective management and development of people at work. For full details of all our titles please telephone the publishing department on 0181 263 3387, fax us on 0181 263 3850, e-mail us on publish@ipd.co.uk, or visit our website on www.ipd.co.uk.

FAST TRACK TO CHANGE

ON THE

HEATHROW EXPRESS

Sue Lownds

INSTITUTE OF PERSONNEL AND DEVELOPMENT

Designed by Curve

Typeset by Paperweight

Printed in Great Britain by The Cromwell Press, Trowbridge, Wiltshire

British Library Cataloguing-in-Publication Data
A catalogue record for this book is available from the British Library

ISBN 0-85292-746-0

The views expressed in this book are the author's own, and
may not necessarily reflect those of the IPD.

**INSTITUTE OF PERSONNEL
AND DEVELOPMENT**

IPD House, Camp Road, London SW19 4UX
Tel.: 0181 971 9000   Fax: 0181 263 3333
Registered office as above. Registered Charity No. 1038333
A company limited by guarantee. Registered in England No. 2931892

Contents

The big picture

Once in a while there emerges an example of organisational change that is remarkable by anyone's criteria.

In June 1998 the Heathrow Express railway opened to the public. This simple statement masks an extraordinary achievement that saw the members of the construction team recover from an enormous and embarrassing setback to participate in a change of culture that has been described as breaking the mould of the UK construction industry.

How did they do it?

▶ They took an approach to teamwork of utter simplicity in its concept and sheer practical good sense in its implementation, yet spirited and pioneering in turning convention on its head.

▶ They made an investment in the development of people that was totally driven by the recognition that individuals will often need individual help, not set programmes.

▶ They adopted an attitude to leadership that is unlike anything I have seen before.

To be right in the middle of such an evolution is a compelling experience. For more than two years Heathrow Express was, for me and my team, an all-absorbing project that taught us, tested us and thrilled us all at once. We found there invaluable lessons about behavioural change that can be applied anywhere.

We were a group of external consultants, but our approach to the programme of culture change is just as applicable to internal change facilitators. Success is not a feature of external or internal status, but of personal drive, team organisation, real conviction in our role and a huge enjoyment of working with people – qualities that can be found in abundance within your own staff.

I offer you our story in the conviction that it will generate lively debate in your own organisations. More than that, I fervently hope that you will find here a helpful store of practical ideas to apply in your own circumstances, drawn from real-life experience in a change programme that was down-to-earth and rooted in the everyday realities of human behaviour and human relationships.

Sue Lownds,
June 1998

Before we start...

I ask you to bear in mind that the terms I use in this book worked for us in the context in which we were operating. I do not seek to imply that our choice of language would suit you and your own unique organisations. Yet the ideas and messages behind the terminology are likely to strike a chord with you and to line up with many of your own experiences. I expect, however, that you will customise our language to whatever is appropriate for your own circumstances and preferences.

I would also like to emphasise that although, for author's convenience, I refer to my team as 'change facilitators', when at work we would not have been recognised by this title because we were known to our colleagues simply by our first names.

You will find the terms 'change leader', 'change facilitator' and 'change influencer' regularly used. This is a convenient way to differentiate between the main influencers I have found in change programmes.

▶ The term 'change leader' is applied to the senior managers who decide upon, instigate, and represent a course of change.

▶ The term 'change facilitator' is applied to those who are formally charged with implementing specific elements of a change programme.

▶ The term 'change influencer' is applied to anyone who assists the process of change formally or informally.

▶ The term 'change programme' is applied to an intended and planned investment in shifting attitudes and behaviour, such as the change in the Heathrow Express construction project from an adversarial to a co-operative and collaborative approach.

▶ The term 'culture change' is applied to that marked change in the personal behaviour of individuals that alters the feel and atmosphere of a workplace – such as the change from withholding information to sharing it, from bawling out to finding out, and from a readiness to blame to a willingness to trust.

Acknowledgements

This book is dedicated, with admiration, to everyone who played a part in the construction of the Heathrow Express Railway; to my husband and kindred spirit, Ken Lownds, who spent hours and hours co-developing and crystallising the philosophy and ideas we applied at Heathrow Express and who personally guided the implementation of these ideas in practice; and to our team who worked alongside us at different stages of the project and brought to this assignment their enthusiasm and their energy – Anne, David, Frances, Karen, Kip, Sharon and Stella.

THE DIPPER'S GUIDE

(A summary of the book for quick reference)

This book is in two main sections – *Truth at the Top* and *Into the Cracks*. The case snapshots that start these sections offer practical evidence and real-life examples of behavioural change. Each case illustration is then followed by a description of the principles behind the practice.

Truth at the Top focuses on the behaviour of senior managers as an invaluable example for others.

Into the Cracks describes the painstaking follow-through that is needed for sustained change.

Truth at the Top – a summary

The first critical factor for a successful change of culture is:

Invest first and foremost in the top team.

Their behaviour is so powerful a role model that it deserves the most thorough and personal attention of all.

If necessary, use independent change facilitators to help every senior manager to master the change of behaviour for him- or herself, demonstrating that the desired change has been applied at a very individual and practical level to the top team: a potent example to others and an investment that will reward you many times over.

Case snapshot

The case snapshot from the Heathrow Express construction project describes the critical factors that distinguish a senior management team that has genuinely immersed itself in culture change – backing up oral agreement of the desired change with unmistakable examples of team members' own change of behaviour. The critical factors are:

▶ personal support and close *involvement* in the activities of the change programme

▶ the use of change facilitators as personal *coaches*

▶ the use of a *language* that was radically different from the language to which people were accustomed.

Chapter 3 – The balancing act

An overview of a number of approaches to help the senior management team master the culture within its own ranks. These are amplified in the chapters that follow. The starting-point is the recognition that senior managers are subject to the same human imperfections as the rest of us, and that an analysis of their own strengths and weaknesses helps them to line up their qualities, as change leaders, in the most shrewd and effective way.

Chapter 4 – Crystallising

The change leaders put together their view of behavioural change not just as a concept but with practical examples of why and how exactly the behavioural change, commencing with their own change of conduct, will benefit the organisation and its people.

Chapter 5 – Personalising

In a private process of self-analysis, the members of the senior team apply the words to themselves, comparing how well they really meet the standards of behaviour they wish to see in the organisation at large. This is an intense and highly personal discipline of facing reality, which can be supported by the use of an independent change facilitator acting as a coach. The outcome of this activity is, firstly, a set of behavioural standards that the change leaders then apply to themselves, and, secondly, the evolution of a process for giving feedback to each other.

Chapter 6 – Organising

Recognise the human reality that we do not all possess exactly the right skills at exactly the optimum level. Some members of the senior management team will not be able to deliver all the time. So they plan for this and cover for each other – for example, through agreeing an 'unofficial' organisation of critical 'cells' with complementary behaviour.

Chapter 7 – Characterising

The visible behaviour of senior managers will sway others to a real step-change. The wisest change leaders find ways to capitalise on this powerful source of influence by means of thoughtful conduct, sustained (not piece-meal) involvement in the various activities of a change programme, and the courage to use language that breaks the mould.

Into the Cracks – a summary

Acknowledge the reality that people will need to be convinced and helped in different ways. Take the time and thought to put together a team of change facilitators who are comfortable adapting themselves to the whole range of demands they will meet, and can apply themselves with variety and responsiveness out and about in the field to influence others to make the desired adjustment. This personal attention is absolutely crucial to making a difference and *sustaining* it.

It is a pity to see so many change programmes that start off magnificently peter out because of the lack of investment in real follow-through into every corner of the organisation. *Into the Cracks* describes the patience, the persistence, and the personal touch that will make this happen.

Case snapshot

This case snapshot from the Heathrow Express construction project provides an insight into what it meant to be a change facilitator on this assignment. The composition of the team of change facilitators affected the approach to the change programme, and their personal motivation was a vital element of their success as influencers of others. About 70 per cent of change facilitators' time in this project was devoted to behind-the-scenes, personal coaching of key influencers. The quality of the relationships that individual change facilitators built with people of all levels, the degree of recharging time built into the assignment, and the versatility and innovation of the change facilitators were all high contributing factors to this programme of behavioural change.

Chapter 8 – Gold dust

The sustainability of a change programme rests to a very large degree on the qualities of the change facilitators who will be working day by day among the people of the organisation. The skills of communication and influencing are only part of the picture.

Among the most significant of the facilitators' qualities are personal resilience in the face of a demanding range of responsibilities and their tolerance of uncertainty. They owe it to themselves and to their sponsor to devise a process for recharging their batteries, for example, through building into the programme periods of time away from the assignment. These 'time aways' will sustain their motivation and allow them to bring back to the project new perspectives and ideas.

Chapter 9 – Working the wheel

One of the most important characteristics of change facilitators is the alertness and openness of mind that leads them to one of the most effective of all activities in a change programme: one-to-one, detailed coaching of key influencers.

Chapter 10 – Thinking triggers

Change facilitators can help themselves by lining up their allies at a very early point in the programme. Allies will be found among those at the front line as well as among management, and the clues are to be found in the language that people use and in their response to and participation in the programme's activities. When you find them, your allies may need training or coaching to help them to reach a level of comfort and effectiveness, but it is an investment that is well worthwhile, and enables the change facilitators to achieve that most gratifying activity of transferring their skills and knowledge to others.

Chapter 11 – Working with the grain

If change facilitators take the time and thought to vary their approach, they will find themselves tapping into a rich source of support. There are three different levels of facilitation they could apply. Choice of activity is likely to be determined by the quality of the relationships that change facilitators have been able to develop with others, the nature of their own skills, and their flexibility.

OPPORTUNITY'S ODYSSEY

The traveller and the horse

'A good horse,' said the traveller,
'Wise man,' said the horse.
But the journey's success
Needs both to hold course.

A proverb for organisations on the move

1

On the move

Every organisation is on the move in some way: changing shape, changing style, changing skills. The pace of change is a fact of life everywhere – in businesses, government, educational institutions, family life, social structures and even, these days, in convents and religious houses. Think of the terms we hear and read all around us – mission statements, change visions, change agents, facilitative management, virtual teams. They are all elements of organisations on the move.

This book casts its attention on a specific kind of change that is burgeoning in all manner of organisations – the value and emphasis being placed on what have come to be known as 'soft' issues. Soft issues, in this volume, are defined as all those interpersonal and behavioural skills, those mentalities and attitudes that profoundly affect not only the internal atmosphere of an organisation but also the manner in which an organisation interacts with other organisations: how people talk to each other, for example, how they listen, how people react to new initiatives, how they influence others, how flexibly they work, and how thoughtful or helpful or truthful they are.

Often, organisational change is greeted with apprehension or incomprehension because it is accompanied by the need for individuals to change their behaviour, to leave behind conventional attitudes, or to alter the mindsets that have been a source of reassurance and comfort. This book explores the practical elements that can make organisational change fulfilling and fruitful at an individual and team level, as well as a tool for financial and organisational performance.

What is said in these pages is both self-evident and subtle. Many of you will recognise the issues and the terminology. Some of the statements and definitions will be obvious. But the pertinent personal qualities and disciplines that underpin them are not. This book has been written because, whereas the language of change is used freely (and at times misused), and the principles of change are often readily espoused, it is not obvious to organisations how to achieve real and sustainable change in the detailed, specific, everyday behaviour of people – whether senior managers or front-line staff.

For this reason, I have made an actual story the focal point of this book to demonstrate the scope, characteristics and potential

Heathrow Express is a compelling story that offers valuable insights

of behavioural change. This is not intended to imply that Heathrow Express represents a perfect example of a change programme in action and, indeed, I have drawn on other examples too. But it is a compelling story, it offers practical evidence that supports my points, and, most importantly, it offers valuable insights into what might have been done better.

The text is interspersed with general frameworks and there is a section of *Take-Away Tips* for you to adapt to your own circumstances. *Case snapshots* from the Heathrow Express construction project are offered to provoke you to think and to generate debate on the personal disciplines, effort, and qualities that are needed by those involved in leading or influencing change. *Food for thought* learning-points highlight what could have been done better – including what I personally could have done better. There were, of course, processes and structures, policies and legal arrangements that contributed to the culture of this project. This book, however, concentrates on the people issues and on the behavioural change that made such a difference.

I hope you will find, as I did, that the story of this particular change programme is a rich learning opportunity. It is certainly one that helped me gain conviction in the common-sense solutions we applied. I hope you will also find that these can be transferred readily into your own workplace. Perhaps, too, it will be a chastening reminder that, however obvious it may seem, people simply do not apply (without a lot of personal encouragement, guidance and reassurance) what their own experience has told them about their personal behaviour and the behaviour of others, and so they and their organisations miss out on their unharnessed potential. However, find a way to tap into that potential, and you have an organisation on the move – really on the move.

2

The three realities

The reality of time

Time pressures – one of the realities of life for so many of us. If you labour under this particular reality, the *Dipper's Guide* at the front of the book is especially for you, because it acknowledges that lack of time can often influence our own reading behaviour, so that we find ourselves dipping and skipping. So, the *Dipper's Guide* will enable you to take a quick dip into the gist of the philosophy and the real-life case examples, along with chapter references for more detailed reading later.

For each of the ideas in the book I could have added any number of words. I have exercised restraint, however, in order to supply as uncluttered and down-to-earth an insight into what is, after all, not a theoretical matter, but the intensely practical process of influencing the behaviour of others.

The reality of human nature

This book is also for those influencers of culture within organisations who have their feet planted firmly in another reality – the reality of human nature. These pages address the significance of emphasising the value of soft skills in working life. The reality of human nature is that some of us are open-minded and some of us are not, some of us are responsive and some of us are not, some of us will be on one wavelength and some of us on quite another. That is part of the tantalising richness as well as the intractable reality of working life, and the most effective influencers of behavioural change are those who find their own personal ways to galvanise the galaxy of individual characteristics and mindsets.

There are two main sections in the book. *Truth at the Top*, on the significance of the role of senior managers, is addressed to 'change leaders' as the initiators of a programme of planned change as well as to those who are in a position to influence them. *Into the Cracks* is written from the perspective of my team of change facilitators, and offers the lessons of practical experience and insight that we hope will assist others who are involved in the process of influencing behaviour in organisations.

The reality of determined perseverance

Although we offer you suggested approaches and frameworks, you will also find here a realistic optimism that stresses the significance of resolute commitment and purposeful, thoughtful action at an individual and detailed level, because models and frameworks will not of themselves reach out to the individuals who will make the

The diversity of human relationships cannot be crammed into boxes

difference to your organisation. The diversity of human relationships, the complexity of human behaviour, and the surprises of human attitudes cannot be crammed into convenient boxes. To carry on as though they do is to dupe yourself with false comfort and to position yourself for disappointment.

But what models cannot do, you can. Change in organisations can mean a whole range of adjustments: a fresh focus on relationships with internal and external customers, a different set of processes, a new way of organising ourselves, or an emphasis on personal accountability. Behind any of these strategies lies the determining factor between success and failure – the practical behaviour of real people. So, if genuine change rather than political pretence is needed, no model, however attractive, catchy or easily absorbed will release you from the investment you will need to make in developing the behavioural skills of your people at a very personal and detailed level, starting with the very top echelons of organisational life.

TRUTH AT THE TOP

The crab and his mum

A crab said to her son, 'Why do you walk sideways like that? You ought to walk straight.'

'If you show me how, mother,' said the son, 'I'll follow your example.'

Aesop on the value of role models and practising what we preach

Case snapshot I

To emphasise the value of behavioural change as a *practical tool* for organisational efficiency, I have chosen to offer you first the practical experience of Heathrow Express, and then the philosophy and guidelines that lay behind the practice.

The description of the key aspects of senior management style and mentality that enabled the programme of culture change at Heathrow Express to start up and, more significantly, to endure raises questions about the reason we do not see evidence of this particular management approach more often in senior teams.

The chapters that follow this case discussion analyse the qualities and activities that distinguish the behaviour of senior managers who are *genuinely* and deeply involved in encouraging real change.

The difference is...

The change of culture during the construction of the Heathrow Express Railway was marked – indeed, extraordinary. It succeeded in moving this particular group of construction operators away from the conventions of the UK construction sector, which has been accustomed to relationships that have more to do with conflict than with harmony. Associations between customer and contractor, between contractor and supplier, and between supplier and supplier are frequently marred by claims and litigation that have largely been accepted as the normal way of conducting oneself in a construction project – until now. Despite the calamitous collapse of the railway tunnel in the centre of Heathrow Airport which, in a traditional construction project, would have seen client and contractor spurring their lawyers to action in a divisive struggle, *this* contractor and *this* client discarded convention and, instead, drew closer together to overcome the catastrophe.

Of all the noteworthy features of this programme of culture change, one of the most remarkable characteristics was the depth and degree of the personal investment made by some of the project's most senior managers in the actual day-to-day 'cultural' activities. This made a huge difference to the success and sustainability of the programme. Some of these managers immersed themselves in aspects of the programme in a manner that, in my experience, is truly rare among senior managers, embracing the kinds of activities a great many senior teams would view as better delegated to others in order to preserve the value of their own time.

Regular contact with the front line, regular contact with suppliers at all levels (including planned visits made by directors to the premises of suppliers – not to discuss technicalities, but to introduce the concept of the new culture), and constant contact with individuals at all levels and with teams at all levels were all intrinsic elements of the behaviour of the change leaders at

Heathrow Express. They were a feature of a management attitude that astutely differentiated between information (the one-dimensional emphasis on facts and data) and real understanding (getting the measure of people – the multi-dimensional 'feel' of people as they really are in the workplace, complete with their emotions, their hunches, their anxieties, their insights, their work experiences, and their natural wisdom).

Information is what we obtain from attitude surveys (something that, incidentally, we chose not to undertake on this project because we saw them as neither potent enough nor personal enough for the approach we had adopted). Understanding is what we obtain from genuine contact. And the significance of the difference? Influencing others is considerably augmented by being able to 'tune into' their preferences: what turns them off or on, their motivations, their preferred use of language, their dislikes, their values, and the quality of their relationships with others within their own organisation or in the other organisations with which they deal.

I would like to offer you an insight into what this all meant in practice. As you read through this case snapshot and the other later in the volume, keep in mind the question, 'Why do we not see more evidence of this kind of "soft" behaviour from the most senior managers in organisations?' Is it perhaps because:

▶ its impact and its contribution to business or organisational success is undervalued, or overlooked, or misunderstood

▶ we are too locked into conventions about the manner in which senior managers should conduct themselves

▶ the translation of theory to actual behaviour is more of a challenge than initially it may appear?

The chapters that follow the case snapshots will seek to analyse the elements that enabled such a significant step-change in people's attitudes and behaviour, and will explain the philosophy behind our chosen approach, a philosophy so sharply and palpably crystallised in this particular change programme.

Background on the construction of the Heathrow Express railway

The construction of the railway involved three principal stages:

▶ the construction of the tunnels and stations

▶ the construction of the track work

▶ the fitting out and commissioning of the whole system.

Over 100 separate supplier and contractor organisations were involved in the project.

A significant aspect of this particular construction project was the crucial nature of the logistics. The construction was taking place primarily beneath the world's busiest international airport. In addition, the need for a linear approach to construction – one major contractor following another for the different phases of the construction – required immense co-ordination to work successfully.

In October 1994, the project suffered an enormous setback when the tunnel in the central terminal area of Heathrow Airport collapsed. It was a critical time for everyone involved, and was the juncture at which BAA plc, the owner of Heathrow airport, chose not to pursue the traditions of the construction industry, which would have meant seeking legal and financial compensation. Instead, their choice of a construction director who would pursue and influence a level of co-operation not usually seen in the UK construction sector resulted in a project that, despite the delays and setbacks of the collapse, reduced by 20 per cent the costs it expected to carry after the collapse, made up critical construction time, and saw the opening date for the railway brought forward from early 1999 to June 1998. The Heathrow Express construction project remodelled the way such construction projects can work, incorporating every organisation in the project and even, in a truly far-sighted move, funding the training and development of its own chain of suppliers. It needed vision, influence, co-operation, and an innovative programme.

The need for a linear approach to construction required immense co-ordination to work

The programme of culture change

By the end of 1995, when my involvement in the project commenced, the senior team was already largely in place and the technical recovery from the collapse of the tunnel was underway. A new contract between the customer (BAA plc) and its major contractor at the time heralded a changed client–contractor relationship and a different way of working. The expression 'the seamless team' was beginning to be heard, though it was the subject of scoffing ridicule and sarcastic send-ups in the early days from some who claimed to have seen it all before, or who were troubled by the signs of change. It was a sad indication of the depth of the rut into which sometimes we can allow ourselves to be driven.

Nevertheless, the phrase 'seamless team' expressed a clearly stated hope for close collaboration and co-operation between the various parties involved in the construction of the railway. The Health and Safety Executive (HSE) had started its investigation into the collapse, the repercussions of which were evident in the caution and heightened wariness of many of those I met.

It was in this atmosphere of uncertainty that my team of change facilitators was set the assignment of fostering and developing, as quickly as possible, attitudes and behaviour that demonstrated that the 'seamless team' was not just a fine phrase but could be seen in action all around the project. Specifically, we were to influence attitudes away from rivalry and towards cohesion, moving from an 'organisational' to a 'cross-organisational' mentality. In the context of the dented morale and the uncertainty that prevailed, an approach that was temperate and restrained rather than bells and whistles seemed a sound choice, both for us and for the senior management team.

As we set about our work, we found ourselves in the midst of a plethora of mixed responses and emotions: honesty and hostility, welcome and avoidance, support and derision. Resistance to change is not unexpected, but the vehemence of reaction can be. Nonetheless the back-up that came from our sponsor, the construction director, and many of his senior team offered us a firm foothold and sustained support.

The difference is...four crucial agreements

There were four agreements, some of them unspoken, between us and our sponsor. These were, without doubt, the paramount factors that underpinned our work.

First, we had the unequivocal and *unswerving support* of our sponsor, the construction director, who never denied or prevaricated over any request we made for his personal involvement or intervention at critical junctures or significant points of the change programme, even if this meant rearranging his packed diary.

Second, the alliance between us, the supplier, and the sponsor was an *alliance based on concept* (the desired change), not detail (pre-ordained activities). This was absolutely crucial because it was a recognition, very early on, of two important aspects of a behavioural change programme:

▶ that the change facilitators, chosen after all for their combined and individual skills and judgement, could be trusted to use those skills and that judgement to respond to whatever they met

▶ that the programme would evolve according to the needs of this particular environment and this particular group of people.

Right from the start, we dispensed with 'boxes' and pre-programmed rituals to give people the space and respect to develop in the ways that suited them, not us. In circumstances of such versatility and fluidity, the degree of trust between the sponsor and the change facilitators, and the synergy of the wavelength on which both parties operate, are fundamental to the whole operation and deserve careful exploration before setting out. In this case they happened to be factors that had been determined by previous work relationships.

Third, there was a commitment from the beginning to a *sustained effort*, acknowledging that one of the critical success factors in a behavioural change programme is the nature, quality and duration of the relationship between the change facilitators and others.

Lastly, we sat *outside the organisational hierarchy*, holding no formal position or title. We had no established desk or office. We had no authority or jurisdiction over anyone, relying entirely on our ability to influence. We worked on a *part-time* basis and moved around sites to establish links, to make contacts and to develop relationships. One person described us as the 'ether', because we seemed to be everywhere and nowhere. This may sound daunting. In fact it was invigorating and expedient, as I shall explain.

The difference is...the behaviour of senior management

These factors, implicit or explicit, were the framework for change. Behind this framework lay the behaviour of the senior managers. This formed the solid foundation from which flowed the activities that influenced the attitudes of others. Every senior manager was involved at some point and in some way – at the scouting events that prefaced every new phase of the project, at 'question time' sessions, and at group discussions. This is not to say that all the senior managers conducted themselves with the same verve or conviction, but overall they communicated an important message for others.

In many change programmes the most senior people introduce the philosophy and allow others to immerse themselves in the implementation and re-inforcement. In this programme, the senior team was an integral part of the implementation, the degree of involvement depending on personal style and personal skill, the change facilitators frequently approaching those managers on whose particular attributes they felt they needed to draw. So, for example, many managers would be invited to some events (such as the 'bring a boss' forum to exchange views and information), three or four of the most key decision-makers might be invited to a 'question time' session with the front-line staff, and perhaps only one or two of them, because of their skills and mentality, might be utilised for an advanced team-building session or as co-facilitators on a particular training workshop. Our choice was based on our experience of the different managers. Acceptance of the principle of accommodating each other's styles meant that only rarely was any offence taken, and it was helpful not to be overburdened and distracted by the need to prop up egos.

Throughout the project there was no slackening in the dissemination of the basic message: that, regardless of our organisational affiliations, we were not competing with each other but operating as one team, with overriding loyalty to the goal of delivering the railway. At each major gathering or seminar the principles of trust and co-operation that underlined the philosophy of the change programme were iterated and reiterated.

We were one team, with overriding loyalty to delivering the railway

The difference is...the choice of language

For change leaders, 'living' the change on a daily basis is perhaps the most taxing of all aspects of a change programme, requiring the mustering of personal resources and the kind of attention to personal behaviour that make the continuous example of individual change leaders the most convincing and authoritative of teachers. One of the very best illustrations I can offer you from the Heathrow Express project is the way language was used. Language is such a crucial influencing tool, yet it is surprising how often its significance is overlooked. There are two demonstrations below of the influence of language.

The words of the construction director exemplify the need for a thick skin and a firm eye on the goal. He speaks about one of the aspects that most tested him in the change of culture and mindset from rivals to 'seamless team' when he arrived at Heathrow Express. Bear in mind the litigious propensity of the UK construction industry and the sometimes belligerent environment in which this language was used. Then consider its impact, the likely responses of those who first heard it, and the tenacity it took to keep using such language in the face of the mockery that initially followed it and that I witnessed for myself.

The words of the senior contractor, an individual who carried a reputation for grapple and gristle, are an illustration of the power of seemingly contrasting attributes: the readiness to take on even the most difficult issues and the sense, subtlety and sensitivity to take in what others have to say. (Interestingly, he emphasises the 'soft' skill of listening not only to what is spoken but also to what is *not* spoken.)

The construction director and the language of influence

Here are the words of the construction director:

— The one word I would choose as most significant for me in this programme of culture change is *trust*. It is such an easy word to say and such a difficult quality to achieve. The key is in the behaviour of the most senior people. Engendering real trust has always been a priority at every stage of my involvement. It has required constant re-inforcement. I see this as a critical feature of leadership.

— *What do you mean by 'real trust'?*

— I mean that the *conduct as well as the words* of the senior team are such that it positively affects the behaviour of others. For example, when some of our people asked us to invest in an extra shift so that we could speed up the work in a crucial area of construction, the senior team listened to their reasoning, then took the decision to trust their judgement. The cost of the extra shift was £130,000, but we ended up saving 12 weeks of valuable construction time and steered a course to earlier opening and earlier revenue. If you remember that the projected weekly revenue from the railway is £1.2 million, it puts the investment of £130,000 in context.

Trust was also at the heart of our decision to reduce the number of quantity surveyors through single team-working, especially in an industry that is so used to the adversarial way of doing business. But trust had to be reinforced through some supportive training and team-building, and even one-to-one help for some of the individuals.

Trust is the basis for our scouting meetings – when we look ahead to each new phase of the project. At our early scouting meetings, fear of reprisal meant people would present a rosy picture, and we found out much later than we should have done about potential show-stoppers.

We were working against the whole tradition of the construction industry

This was where we were, in effect, working against the whole tradition of the construction industry: owning up to problems would in other projects have been the basis for legal letters or legal action and financial claims. On this project we really have worked at ensuring people don't get penalised for flagging up issues of concern.

The senior managers have tried to stay close to the front line in all kinds of ways – by regular walkabouts or by responding to invitations for specific involvement in some of the cultural activities. For example, one of the change facilitators asked if I would be willing to act as a 'mentor' to a site foreman who had expressed an interest in understanding the way senior managers look at things on this project. Some people may view this as inappropriate use of a director's time, but I think it is precisely this kind of contact that ensures we do not lose touch with the real issues and, more importantly, with the very people on whom we rely to deliver the promises that we, at senior management level, make to our customers.

— *How difficult has it been to turn the prevailing culture round?*

— The process of changing the culture to these soft skills has not been easy, and it was by no means completely achieved. I can remember that when I started to talk about a 'no-blame' culture even some of my senior colleagues misunderstood. I was criticised for fostering an attitude of no accountability, when, in fact, what I was seeking to influence was an attitude of mind that said 'We do not seek blame, we seek the cause.' It needed constant statement and re-statement before it began to be understood. People also needed to see that I could personally be challenged and that it did not affect their place or position on the project. I've had to take on board some very personal criticisms. One of the people on whom I can wholly rely not to mince her words is my secretary. As a result of her insights I have built 'relationship' time into my diary in order to get to know well the people around the patch who might not normally come into contact at all with a director, and I have found myself apologising to people with whom I might have dealt too roughly (something which, I'll confess, does not always come easily to me).

We did not get to complete and total trust on this project, I'll admit that, even though we have seen some great successes, such as the remarkable outcome of one 'single' commercial team working really closely, where usually there would be a commercial team made up of duplicate quantity surveyors and finance guys who all keep watch over each other in the expectation that someone is trying to rip off someone else.

We have also seen the evolution of a number of mechanisms through which to foster trust – from the very large forums that have been held just a handful of times to bring together 40 or 50 key people to air all the angles of a particular issue, to 'prayer meetings' held at the start of each day, to one-to-one trouble-shooting sessions.

The contractor and the language of influence

Here are the words of one of the most senior managers on the Heathrow Express construction project. He identified three attitudes of mind that contribute to the effectiveness of a senior manager in the midst of change:

▶ staying in context

▶ staying cool

▶ staying in contact.

This is what he said to us:

— *What do you do to stay in context?*

— It's important to think context the whole time – the big picture. If you think context, you'll realise that most problems are little, and early tackling keeps them little. Heathrow Express issues were an aggravation, not major problems. That is not to say that they were not important. Heathrow Express had massive logistics and programme issues, and the biggest single issue was convincing the Health and Safety Executive that we could restart work and do it in an appropriate manner.

But it is the attitude of senior managers that can contain those issues or convert them into major blocks. If you let one problem overexcite you and overwhelm you today, you lose confidence tomorrow. If you lose your own self-confidence, you are of absolutely no use to your staff.

Retaining your self-confidence is a feature of keeping everything in context. We may be the official leaders, but we are not infallible, and quite often (in fact more often than not) it is the experience and knowledge of others that will see you through. You just have to listen and take note, and not be hung up about loss of face or status.

Your attitude will determine how well you listen, and how well you listen will determine whom you use to trouble-shoot or to organise or motivate others, and when to take a risk or two.

— *What do you mean exactly by 'staying cool'?*

— Staying cool when all around are losing their cool is a real differentiator in a project leader – in any time-bound project, not just a construction one. That means keeping your cool when there is a problem to resolve. Keeping your cool is also risking a guy in a critical post he has never ever done before. Keeping your cool is inviting people to challenge your point of view and not taking it personally.

Keeping cool is really risk-taking with a safety net, and the safety net has everything to do with how well you listen. For example, some would say I was taking a risk when I put a particular guy in charge of a significant logistics operation in the tunnel. He hadn't done anything like it before, but he was not afraid to challenge me on the way things were organised. So I told him to have a go and put his money where his mouth was. But the safety net was that I had already walked around and taken a good look at how he had organised his team and organised his part of the job, and it was the cleanest, neatest and most organised. I also listened to how others talked about him and knew how he was viewed by the tunnel gangs, and I knew, because of the kind of guy he was, that he would come to me if he needed help. So – risk with a contingency determined by how well you listen.

— *Why is it so necessary to stay in contact?*

— Close contact with your people and with your suppliers is absolutely critical. Without it how can you possibly know and understand what is bugging them or working well for them? How can you help in the most appropriate way? And how can you begin to identify the talent that is worth an investment? There are so many ways to keep in contact.

The monthly 'Suppliers Club' on the Heathrow Express project has been a great forum for contact. We circulate, we chat, we pick up information and give information, we re-establish contact. The format is half information and half socialising – updates on different parts of the project from management, suppliers and so on, and then a buffet dinner and a social close to the event. An opportunity to listen.

The scouting meetings held at the start of each phase of the project help everyone who is going to be part of that phase to make contact with each other, to get to know each others' technical expertise and track record, and to get to know each other personally as an aid to later communication. It's a time to listen, to look ahead, to think ahead and to plan ahead – *together*.

Close contact means that people are more likely to challenge you. I don't like people who just say yes. It gets awful lonely out there, and you can make a lot of mistakes if people don't give you feedback. But there is a difference between challenging and insubordination. Challenging is, let's say, when you bring a group of people together to knock about a particular problem, you encourage them to come up with solutions, you encourage them to challenge the solutions, and you ask all there if they will support the chosen solution, or to challenge it and say why. Insubordination is when they fail to challenge or object, and then go out and do something different.

It is the duty of the person in charge to keep listening in order to be aware of everyone who is contributing. Sometimes you get 'group think': everyone goes along with a course of action just because one strong influencer has suggested it. Quite often I will wander along to someone's office after a meeting and say, 'I notice you were quite quiet in there. Is there something about our decision that is bugging you?' And we explore any objections. I consider it my personal responsibility to ensure there is 'buy-in': it isn't about keeping every person happy but it *is* about not wasting valuable time. The greatest plan in the world has failed because one person did it differently. Even if you get it wrong, you can at least analyse why you got it wrong, because you know everyone did what was agreed – otherwise you'll never know if your decision was right or wrong.

The significance of the role played by key managers like these on the Heathrow Express construction project cannot be overestimated. Nor can their unselfconscious use of 'soft' language like 'trust' and 'no blame', 'listening' and 'close contact'.

It occurs to me that the ease with which I have been able to commit to paper this first case snapshot is in sharp contrast with the intense effort and commitment needed to alter a culture. The sustained and detailed involvement of the most senior managers on the project was unlike anything I have witnessed on other change programmes. Why is this level of participation from senior managers not seen more often, given its undoubted and powerful impact on others?

The analysis in the next few chapters of the key elements that differentiate full and genuine involvement from an involvement that is short-lived, sporadic or irresolute will serve to demonstrate the nature and extent of the dedication, diligence and application needed. There is also a number of suggested activities that could be used to help a team of change leaders to master its own culture.

3
The balancing act

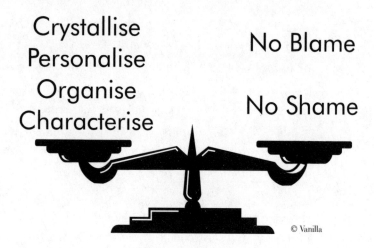

Crystallise
Personalise
Organise
Characterise

No Blame

No Shame

© Vanilla

If there is one crucial element to a successful programme of behavioural change, it is the example from the very top (board members, directors, general managers, heads of functions or departments and so on). It is curious that organisations will invest in drastic changes, such as mergers and downsizing or re-organising and restructuring, without linking that change to the vital behavioural qualities of their most prominent role models. The 'soft' or 'interpersonal' skills of their most senior managers are, too often, either *assumed* to be present or are considered too difficult an area to tackle even when they are patently not present.

Many of you will have worked in organisations that agonise about the value of an investment in soft skills while making gigantic investments in other changes that demand the very highest level of interpersonal skill of those whose task it is to explain, introduce, support, and re-inforce that change. The example of the senior management role model is so very powerful in fostering real change that it is short-sighted not to invest in the personal behaviour of the top team.

When the speed of change is critical, as it was on the construction of the Heathrow Express railway, the example from the top supplies the kind of head-start for which there is no substitute.

The behaviour of your key managers will make the difference between success and failure and between transition or termination. Anything less than total commitment to the cause that they, after all, will usually have initiated, anything less than daily demonstration of the behaviour that will support the principles and philosophy of the change programme will be perceived as insincere and ineffective. But the senior team that is seen, without exception, to have changed its own behaviour will outstrip expectations, win over the waverers and neutralise the 'well-poisoners'. The greater the change, the greater the need for this example from the top. They are the epicentre.

When the senior team view their responsibilities as being *the guardians of an organisation 'on the move'*, it affects their own attitude and their own behaviour, because nurturing an adaptive mentality in their people then becomes an integral, vital and continuous part of a senior manager's role, not an additional or peripheral function to the 'real job', or an activity to be relegated or delegated.

The issue for the leaders of a behavioural change programme is that too often in our analytical, action-oriented, and measurement-based organisations the behavioural implications are seen as difficult to grasp, difficult to analyse, difficult to explain, evaluate or justify in hard terms,

If the leaders are unconvincing, others falter and fall

and, therefore, difficult to influence or achieve. If the leaders are unconvincing, it is easy for others to falter and fall. If the leaders show conviction, they supply strength, stimulation, and support.

The *Ayes and Noes Balance* can help change leaders to work through this 'too difficult' box. On the left-hand side of the scale are the elements that the senior team commits to *doing*, on the right-hand side, the elements they commit to *not* doing.

1 Crystallise

Crystallise

First in the balance is the way the senior team, as the team of change leaders, visualises change and expresses that vision. This will be determined by their own inclination and belief in their ability to work together to make a difference.

2 Personalise

Crystallise
Personalise

Second in the balance is the way they apply the change *to themselves. How* they use their personal attributes and *how* they support and coach each other will determine their joint ability to inspire others, to re-invigorate flagging spirits, and to convert vision into action. More significantly, it will help them to agree on an appropriate response to those of their team who lack the talent or the appetite to lead the way in behavioural change.

3 Organise

Third in the balance is the way they organise themselves for change – and this will affect their combined effectiveness, their wise use of their multiple skills, their experience, and their restricted time.

4 Characterise

Fourth in the balance is the way they demonstrate – personally and publicly – the change in behaviour they would like to see in others. The way they *live* the change, their choice of conduct – even their choice of language – will affect their ability to influence others to a shared sense of direction.

5 No blame

On the other side of the balance is the avoidance of negative behaviour. 'No blame' does not mean 'no accountability'. In behavioural terms, it means a shift from recrimination and finger-pointing to resolving the mistake and understanding its root cause so that it can be avoided another time. The former approach is time-wasting and alienating. The latter is fruitful and motivating.

6 No shame

This is inextricably linked to 'no blame'. If you are confident that you will not become a scapegoat, you are more likely to acknowledge a mistake and learn from it, rather than hide or deny it. Senior managers have the power and influence actively to discourage the behaviour of damaging ridicule.

At this point, it is important to reflect, in case you should imagine that 'soft' behaviour is timid behaviour, that you cannot indulge in 'no blame' and 'no shame' unless you first admit to, and confront, mistakes. And you cannot move behaviour away from 'blame and shame' unless, without shirking, you tackle evidence of that behaviour head-on.

'No blame, no shame' is not the cowering conduct of the wimp. It is the disciplined action of people with all the mastery of rational argument and all the grit of steely determination.

4

Crystallising

The desired change is expressed as a concept (eg 'We shall work as one team').

Then, a reason is given to explain the move away from the old style, expressed in the context of the organisation's specific circumstances and supported with the weight of the senior team's personal conviction (eg 'We are absolutely sure that replacing our old style of separate teams working towards competing goals with a new style of one team working towards exactly the same goal is better for us and for our business because...').

Finally, the explanation is amplified with practical examples to make it meaningful to the whole range of people in the organisation and, at the same time, assessable by them (eg 'What this means in practice is that at senior management level we shall do a, b, c, at departmental level we shall do x, y, z').

Walking the talk

Senior teams are generally well used to crystallising their vision of change into a plucky mission statement. They are well accustomed to looking forward and gaining agreement on strategic principles, and to encapsulating those principles into public statements on the need, the purpose and the benefits of change. But they are not always much used to adjusting their personal behaviour and their own team behaviour to match their words. And this is the most fundamental of issues for successful culture change.

So, we often see clear evidence of the verbal strategy. We rarely see evidence of the consistent application by senior teams of the wish-statement to *themselves*. Yet it is *their* behaviour that will positively stir up the spirit and the speed of change or, by contrast, irreparably corrode the best efforts of others.

Know what I mean?

When a concept is simple, obvious, and measurable in 'hard' terms, the mission statement needs little explanation. There are some good examples everywhere of unambiguous promises — such as those that vow to courier our parcels or mail within a specific time-scale, come what may. Airlines tell us confidently and precisely the amount of leg room they offer or the size of the seats. 'Soft' skills are rarely simple, however, because they are open to myriad interpretations. What exactly do 'excellent' communication or 'world-class customer service' mean to you? What exactly does 'supportive management' mean to you? What exactly does a 'trusting relationship' mean to you? And are you confident that your understanding matches that of your colleague?

This is why the crystallising phase for a soft-skills change programme needs more than broad statements, however snappy or carefully composed. The nature of the explanation that follows the statement and the examples that are supplied will supplant the cloud of confusion with the comfort of clarity.

Strategists tend to use a thinking style that rapidly connects the links and patterns in an argument so that it makes ready sense to them. The rest of us, however, may need to be helped to see those patterns and links through some graphic, practical, and real-life illustrations. The strategists usually rely on others to do this and, in doing so, miss out on some of their very best opportunities for rapid and redoubtable results.

What a waste...

For example, an investment in soft-skills development is not just about making life more pleasant – though it does! Nor is it just about motivating, delegating, communicating or facilitating, despite the importance to team spirit and team performance of all of those skills. It is also about eradicating waste – the waste of time, effort and emotion that eats into our efficiency. I once worked alongside a manager who kept what he referred to as his 'CYA [cover your a***] Log', which he admitted to updating every day, sometimes for nearly one hour. His rate of pay was £30 an hour, so you can easily work out the cost of this little exercise to protect his back. He did it, however, because he feared the behaviour of his director.

Here lies the hidden cost of aggressive management. How many others were there like him in that organisation? Not only did he consume valuable time in this way, but he would decline to offer any suggestions or ideas to this particular director because of the ridicule he expected to be heaped upon him. Waste of time. Waste of emotion. Waste of energy. Waste of potential.

Don't imagine that it is only an aggressive style that elicits this kind of waste. In a service organisation of excellent reputation, I found a person who had rigged up a system of operating that ensured a particular process took a week to complete rather than the two hours it should have done. The manager of this man was too 'nice' to tackle him, his hesitant management style protected by a culture that valued people who *looked* like they were busy.

In another, equally reputable, organisation, there was the sad spectacle of what came to be known as the 'six o'clock syndrome'. The managing director was known for his walkabouts at 6 pm, during which he had given people the impression that there were credit points to be gained from being seen still beavering away beyond official working hours. So consummate was the need to impress this man, that many of his managers (including some of his directors!) would drape their jackets over their chairs to imply they were still around – and go off to the pub. If the culture of the organisation persuaded such key people to indulge in this kind of deception, what else was being handled dishonestly, silently eating away at organisational effectiveness?

Some of you may be thinking, 'Well, get rid of the wastrels, then, and their managers, if necessary.' Of course that is one strategy – until you examine how much of this kind of behaviour is silently going on (though perhaps less starkly or conspicuously), even right next to you. Far better to engender an environment that makes it unnecessary.

An amplification of vision and strategy, therefore, sometimes needs an intrepid owning-up to the issues that provided the impetus for the strategy in the first place. And that calls for a very special discipline from the strategists, because it requires those responsible for initiating change to be courageous in saying,

Those initiating change must be courageous

publicly, 'This change isn't meant just for you. We are so sure that this change is good that we are going first, starting with ourselves because we see the need to improve our own behaviour as our personal contribution to making this a more effective working environment.' But that isn't all. The next step is to say, 'And this is how *we* shall show that we have changed – and this is the difference we hope it will make to you.'

If senior managers flinch at this, or thwart it through uncertainty or anxiety about their own skills, they can be helped. When they are up to it, however, they have in their grasp the most powerful of all mechanisms for lasting impact. The personalising of change at a senior level adds a robust edge to a change programme and is a towering opportunity for personal growth.

5
Personalising

The desired change is linked solidly to the behaviour of the organisation's leaders. This is a private activity conducted within the senior team so that they can commence the programme with real clarity about the strengths and weaknesses they will carry with them as a team of change leaders.

Associated with this activity is the change facilitator in the role of a personal 'coach', working privately with individual members of the senior management team to help with the process of self-analysis and self-development.

The quality and nature of the relationship between the coaches and those who draw on their services can prove to be one of the most durable and potent of change mechanisms. ('Into the Cracks' (Chapters 8 to 11) will examine this in more depth.)

A change of clothes

The personalising of behaviour will ensure that the exercise is not just a change of clothes for senior managers. Real change may involve some sacrifice for them: letting people in, for example, letting go, letting be. Too often the clothes are renewed while the conduct lags behind – and the mismatch leads others to view the intentions of their leaders as 'lip-service'. Too often the leaders agree readily on the concept but do not apply the behaviour to themselves or to each other, and certainly do not take responsibility for correcting or coaching each other in the new way, or for monitoring and reviewing each other's behavioural performance. Too often the vision of change stops short of determining precisely what the senior team will have to *do* differently to demonstrate that they are serious about change. What do they need to stop doing, start doing, and continue doing?

For a far-reaching, sustainable, meaningful shift of culture, conceptual agreement by the top team is simply not enough. But if it is followed up with detailed scoping of their own behavioural changes, of how precisely they will take responsibility for monitoring, supporting, and coaching each other, and what will happen if one of their number consistently breaks the code of conduct, they will already have achieved that first convincing step-change in adjusting their organisation's culture, because they will be adjusting their own.

This is not as harsh as at first it may appear. These are the standards that organisations often seek to apply to the main body of their people through a performance system, although all too frequently senior managers are themselves exempt. Investment in the top team is the single most significant action in influencing a change of emphasis to soft skills.

What is the nature of this investment? It is diagnostic and specific to each individual. It is personal. And because it is personal it is powerful. It is based on the everyday behaviour of members of the senior team, and that behaviour is re-inforced through the checks supplied by special relationships between the managers and their personal coaches.

The impetus for the Heathrow Express change programme came from a real crisis – the collapse of the railway tunnel in the centre of the world's busiest international airport – and there is nothing like a crisis to focus the mind. The

'No change' was simply not an option

Heathrow Express senior team recognised that the construction industry's conventional reliance on the adversarial way of reprisal and retribution, which would normally have followed such an incident, would not enable the team to deliver the railway in the promised time-scales. For them, 'no change' was simply not an option. They recognised the necessity for the entire group (client, contractors, and suppliers) to work differently – as a single team – in order to achieve. They also recognised the wisdom of offering a level of highly personal support to those who were being asked to work differently, demonstrating that they understood that the change of behaviour needed intensive persuasion and encouragement.

We do not need the catalyst of a momentous incident, however, to spur us on, if only the strategists are prepared to acknowledge that an organisation *not* on the move and not adapting, tuning in to trends and progressing forward actively, as a body, to greet new situations and requirements is already in crisis. For the strategists in this kind of organisation, standing still is actually regressing. It is worth commenting that, although the tunnelling phase of construction on the Heathrow Express had suffered a crisis, the phase that followed it (the fitting-out of the stations and the commissioning of the railway) experienced no such setback. By then, however, the culture of co-operation was seen as good sense and good value, and the supplier organisations in this phase adopted it on this basis alone.

So, this investment in *personal* behaviour entails the categorical and scrupulous agreement by the senior team on what they will do to demonstrate that *they* are behaving differently – not just that they will work as a team to foster change, but *how* exactly what they will be doing will differ from what they currently do, and, most difficult of all, what they will do when someone lacks the skill or the inclination to adhere to the code of conduct. It is an activity that may never be visible to others outside the team, but it sets the most solid of foundations for intelligent and masterful change leadership.

This analysis of their own standards of personal and interpersonal behaviour is something from which many powerful people shrink, perhaps because of a perception that it would lead to loss of face, or perhaps because issues of authority, power, and position mean that teams at the highest levels of organisational life are simply unaccustomed to the kind of appraisal and self-analysis they so often set down as a standard for others. Yet it can be done, with a sensitive touch and a supportive framework, so that it is not seen as beneath dignity or beneath status.

Eagles and turkeys

Convincing others is an all-encompassing activity.

▶ It is no good for a senior team to talk about good communication if they are seen not to be communicating with each other.

▶ It is no good putting out a statement about listening and learning, if the senior team is seen to do neither.

▶ It is no good requiring others not to attack, if the senior managers are aggressive in their own styles.

▶ It is no good talking about the need for teamwork, if you detach yourself from your own team.

I can recall undertaking an assignment for a manager who sat in his splendid office beneath a poster that said 'How can you soar like an eagle when you are surrounded by turkeys?' So absorbed was he by his own sense of humour, he failed to recognise the insult to his team. It is no good talking publicly about the value of personal contact with your people if, as happened with one senior manager of my acquaintance, you are heard to remark that personal contact with fewer than nine or ten people at a time is poor use of your time and of your rank. Certain senior functions – human resources, for example – demand the most exacting standards of all. Those who occupy such functions, and who do *not* embody the behaviour they claim to espouse, are not just prodigal: they are damaging to the organisation. In Ralph Waldo Emerson's words, 'What you *are* speaks so loudly that I can't hear what you *say*.'

Figure 1

TL² – The Behaviour of Culture Leaders

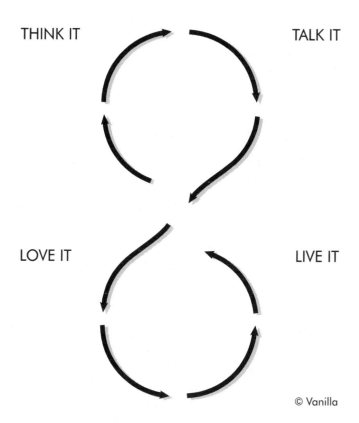

THINK IT   TALK IT

LOVE IT   LIVE IT

© Vanilla

Look at the TL^2 diagram in Figure 1, which describes the behavioural transition of a strong team of culture leaders who move through the quadrants:

▶ thinking about the desired change

▶ talking about what it really will mean

▶ building their enthusiasm for it

▶ demonstrating it.

If they are all in the LIVE IT box, we have the presence, support and power of truly high-quality leadership. But human reality demonstrates how very difficult this is to achieve across the board. There is a way, though, to attain it in those senior teams that are seriously minded to start with themselves. Being seriously minded means that the senior team has acknowledged the value of the whole process (including the self-analysis that accompanies it). The main sponsor of the change programme has a high influencing role at this stage of the proceedings.

The process of facing up to ourselves and facing up to others is an intense and challenging discipline in itself. But there are three ways to achieve it:

▶ firstly, by ensuring that it is as private as possible

▶ secondly, by using the assistance of a personal coach

▶ thirdly, by making up for each other's weaknesses.

(*Note*: I make no apology for the use of the word 'weaknesses'. For some years, those of us involved in the training and development world have been encouraged to utilise the euphemism 'area for development' as a substitute for 'weakness'. Yet having the courage to acknowledge that we have weaknesses is part of the acceptance of human reality and human flaws, even at the top. And why should there be any embarrassment in that?)

Facing up in private

A period of private self-analysis helps each person reflect on his or her own strengths in relation to the qualities required of the whole team as culture leaders. Some people may be able to do this for themselves without a framework or guidance. Others may prefer to work with some structure or with some assistance, or even in pairs or small groups.

If you are invited to offer some assistance to a colleague in this most personal of activities, the indicators that accompany the four quadrants of the TL^2 diagram in Figure 2 (on pages 58–9) offer you some broad prompts to help the process of analysis. But please do remember that the people and the programme will be different on each occasion, and it is wise to develop *specific* indicators that make sense in the context of the particular organisation. It is also wise, at this critical stage, to ensure that the terminology selected for the quadrants does not alienate or antagonise. Words acceptable to one person may cause serious

Figure 2

TL^2 – Indicators of Culture Change

1 Think It

Indicators that tell you a person has thought through the implications of a proposed change:

1   Working through the whole argument (eg 'Why the change?' 'To what extent do I support the change?' 'In what way will the change affect the organisation/ my people/me?' 'What do I actually have to do?')

2   Contingency-planning ('What if...?' scenarios eg 'What if I, personally, cannot deliver x, y, z?')

3   Personal support ('Where are my personal allies?' 'Where and in whom will I be able to place most trust?').

3 Love It

Key indicator that a person has started to do more than talk about it:

Initiating activities of his or her own that will re-inforce the change or take it on another step (ie rather than reacting to the initiative of others).

Figure 2 (continued)

TL² – Indicators of Culture Change

2 Talk It

Indicators that tell you the language of change is being adopted:

1 Language matches the spirit of the intended change

2 Key words used persistently to re-inforce the main messages

3 Management meetings regularly include (a) progress checks on each person's personal contribution to the re-inforcement of change and (b) opportunities to discuss any personal support needed.

4 Live It

Key indicators that a person's behaviour regularly lines up with the change philosophy he or she claims to espouse:

1 Participation in the activities introduced to support the change

2 Daily demonstration of the behaviour implicit in the change

3 Active backing of those who support the process

4 Not shirking opportunities to persuade and influence the cynics and resisters.

disaffection in others. Finally, bear in mind that the indicators alone are of very little use without the art of astute conversation or the faculty of insight, which will serve to draw out what is meaningful and relevant.

The process of personal analysis is hand-on-heart stuff, and part of the ensuing exercise within the senior management team is to challenge evidence of dissembling or self-deception as much as it is to restore balance to diffidence or self-deprecation.

Facing up with a facilitator

The use of a change facilitator in the role of personal coach to prompt and enable this analysis can supply a valuable and invigorating edge to the whole process. The coach sits with each senior manager in order:

▶ to discuss his or her personal style

▶ to differentiate between behaviour that can help or hinder the credibility of the manager as a change leader

▶ to help plot a profile of personal qualities and personal style

▶ to gather evidence to support that profile.

At Heathrow Express I personally took the construction director through a process of analysing his own values and behaviour against the quadrants in the TL^2 diagram. Some people respond comfortably to a formal framework such as this. Others will react with irritation at the very thought of being 'boxed in'. For them, a conversation that works its way subtly and sensitively 'around' the four quadrants is a more effective and unobtrusive mechanism, although this demands from the coach the gift of discourse that is both skilful and ingenious.

It is a time, though, for not mincing words. I was astonished recently to hear a board member of a fairly sizeable and significant organisation confess that he believed himself, at the mere age of 49, to be 'too old to change'. Worse still, he was suggesting to his chairman that the right time for culture change in the organisation would be when the current board had made way for their successors. It reminded me of that curious conversation said to have been overheard between two old people, at the time of decimalisation of the UK currency, who were plaintively pondering why the government simply did not wait until all the old people had died off before introducing decimalisation. If senior people write themselves off with such startling notions, what use are they to others, or to the organisation on the move? The coach of this particular individual would have the task of taking him through a sensitive analysis of the disquiet, distress, or desire that may lie behind his statement before helping him to retune his attitude and his behaviour. In the end, however, it may be time for that board member to bow out with due dignity.

The lead given by senior managers in the use of an internal or external personal coach (or coaches, because each coach will bring a different dimension to the relationship) demonstrates to others that there is no loss of face in so doing. Part of this openness is also to recognise that it may not be possible for every senior manager to demonstrate all of the qualities or skills needed. Senior managers, like the rest of us, are subject to human imperfections, and it is sensible and far-sighted to devise a common-sense system of support to compensate for each other's weaknesses. The result is a senior team working in close co-ordination to line up their behaviour with their wish-statements. It is also a senior team taking very real responsibility for each other's conduct.

Let's not overlook the significance of the attitude that succeeds in accommodating the activity of senior-management coaching.

It is no discredit to be human

It is an attitude that recognises, without shame, that every one of us may need, and can benefit from, support during times of change. It is an attitude that accepts that key managers are at an extreme disadvantage as pioneers of a new way if they allow issues of status to block their own access to the means of developing the personal and interpersonal skills that will play such a crucial part in enabling them to influence that change. It is no discredit to be human.

Facing up to and with each other

Once the private analysis is complete, the sharing of the results with each other has two purposes:

▶ to understand where the greatest strengths of the team exist

▶ to devise a strategy for covering for each other's weaknesses.

I call these the *Honesty in Action* sessions. As one of the senior construction managers on the Heathrow Express project said, 'The greatest plan in the world failed because one person did it differently.' So this is not self-indulgence. It is self-preservation. This phase helps to determine how the change leaders organise themselves to support and sustain the change programme, making best use of their personal attributes and compensating for shortfalls in individual team members.

The style of this phase depends on the degree of openness that already exists in the team and on whether the change has to proceed at an amble or a gallop. Well-established teams may find it easier to work through this than the temporary teams to be found on a construction project, where people have less time to get to know each other because they move in and out of the project and belong to a wide variety of organisations.

For the Heathrow Express senior team, the personal and shrewd interventions of the construction director became the most opportune method of undertaking this sensitive process. By acting as a source of inconspicuous and personal support to individual members of the senior team, he was able to circumvent the fall-out that would have inevitably resulted from an attempt to carry out the personalising process formally. It can be done this way, however, only where the sponsor of change is already operating in the 'Live It' quadrant of the TL^2 diagram, and, therefore, not only refrains from wincing at spending precious time on this activity, but actively and unhesitatingly welcomes it. Otherwise, it is judicious to use an independent change-facilitator to guide the group through this most advanced of team behaviours.

Whether they are 'above the line' sessions, formally structured and facilitated by an independent facilitator, or whether they are 'below the line' sessions that the sponsor of the change programme conducts with a light touch and a low key, this process is a barometer that supplies valuable information on the buoyancy and resolution of those who hold the crucial responsibility of change leadership.

6

Organising

The desired change is taken so seriously that the senior management team plans for the range of demands they will meet. They ensure that two crucial leadership roles – the Prime Mover and the Dedicated Ambassador – are adequately covered by themselves, working in 'cells' or pairs to compensate for shortfalls in the skills of individuals, and to achieve the best balance and exposure for each change leader.

Softly, softly...

The organisation of the change leaders does not have to be public. In fact, public announcements of structure, just like a razzmatazz announcement of change, raise expectations and cynical responses that can work against success. The main purpose of a planned organisation is:

▶ to focus, privately, the strengths of the change leaders

▶ to compensate for shortcomings in the leadership

▶ to agree responsibilities or boundaries that reduce waste of time or effort

▶ to gather the forces of change.

Think functions, not roles

Quite often we make our own lives harder by locking ourselves into a viewpoint that sees roles as held by one person. Why not challenge that viewpoint? Here are two significant roles to support cultural change: the Prime Mover (the sponsor(s) of the change programme) and the Dedicated Ambassador (the contingency role). Remember, these are roles, not titles, and not formal posts. Both entail highly active areas of responsibility distributed within the senior team, who are supported by the behavioural coaches in the field. But they need not be allocated to one person.

Figure 3 shows how much rests on the personal qualities of these roles. Given the reality of human personality, could it not be overoptimistic to expect all of these qualities to be in one person in exactly the degree that is needed? Why not view these roles as *functions*? Once we do this, we can more easily see the function of the Prime Mover as held by more than one person – and we can begin to make it easier on ourselves. It is more attainable to gather together the considerable skills and qualities needed by the Prime Mover or the Dedicated Ambassador if the function is supported by a number of people with complementary strengths.

The Prime Mover

It is better to think in terms of the qualities that this function needs than to try to write a formal task description, which would in all likelihood overlook some of the unexpected angles that sprout up once a change programme is underway. I find it valuable to highlight single words or phrases that build up a graphic picture of the nature, characteristics, disposition, and temperament that define such a function. This constitutes the distinguishing livery of the Prime Mover.

Once we start doing this, it does not take long to see just how demanding a role it is, pin-pointing and encircling seemingly divergent attributes and testing to the limits individual flexibility. Besides, there is a natural tendency to look to the most senior manager as the Prime Mover, and that places considerable pressure on one individual who may have been appointed to his or her post for other reasons than the possession of the complete range of qualities required for the role of Prime Mover. A 'cell' of three or four people can diffuse this situation.

It may be possible to find one individual who represents all that is excellent in each of these qualities. If there is such a person, I suggest that the lead–lag factor between that individual and the rest of the team will prove to be a considerable burden. It is less trying, and certainly less risky, to search for shared capacity. In any case, a cell or unit of Prime Movers has a ready contingency for those occasions when one person will not suffice.

Figure 3

Distinguishing Characteristics of the Prime Mover

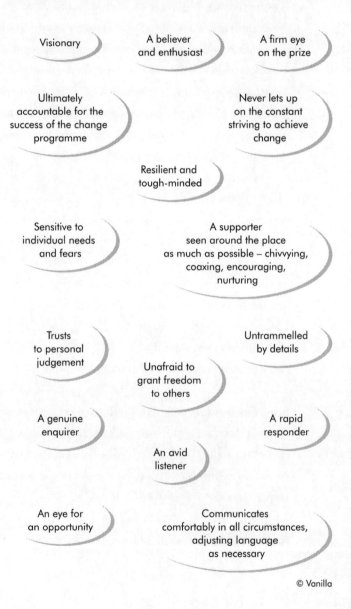

© Vanilla

The Dedicated Ambassador

This is the role of the trusty deputy, standing in for the Prime Mover as necessary so that the change leadership has constant exposure in the arena. The logistics of operational life, and the need for rapid response to differing situations in a range of locations, would tend to lead naturally to a cell of Dedicated Ambassadors backing up the Prime Mover's unit. In addition to the qualities of resilience, enthusiasm, determination, and sensitivity that we need in the Prime Mover, this role also calls for high visibility in the field. This is the roving cultivator of the spirit of change, who notices the details that demand attention or could repay investment. Holding positions of authority in the organisation, the Dedicated Ambassadors can quickly mobilise the support of others. A discerning eye, sound judgement, speed of reaction, and personal integrity are the qualities that define the stature of this role and raise its credibility in the field.

A little reflection highlights the high degree of cohesion, communication, and co-ordination needed for the successful operation of these roles, made simpler when the activity is undertaken by a group of people who have placed their weight so firmly and solidly behind the programme of change that they need no cajoling or coaxing to justify this investment – which is why the thoroughness of the effort in crystallising and per-sonalising is so significant.

7

Characterising

> The change leaders act as real role models for the people of the organisation in demonstrating to others, through their own everyday behaviour, that they have applied the desired change to themselves.

Pause for reflection

I would like to pause here for a caveat. Before we read on, let's remind ourselves that those who 'live it' are not paragons – that would be to place change leaders on an unrealistic pedestal from which they are bound to topple.

Like every other person who struggles to improve, sometimes they will fail to live up to expectations and sometimes they will badly let down those who look to them for inspiration. But they will demonstrate those special qualities of self-awareness and humility that enable them to recognise their failures, learn from them, and strive to do better next time. Most of the time they will be seen as people who are truly striving to keep their behaviour in tune with the philosophy they promulgate.

To show that they can learn, that they can turn back when they are wrong, regardless of issues of position or power or prerogative – these are the differences between a leader we are inclined to admire and support and a leader we tend, privately if not publicly, to disparage and dismiss.

If crystallising the purpose and direction of a change programme is the launch rocket, then its conduct and language – the manifestation of the 'Live It' characteristic – are the twin booster-rockets.

Conduct and the three virtues

There are many facets of conduct that contribute to the impact made by change leaders, from civility to sang-froid. I have found three influences, above all, that single out the conduct of the superior change leader from the merely acceptable. A capacity for generosity, vigilance, and fearlessness are of profound consequence in relating to others.

The virtue of generosity

Generosity often first reveals itself in:

▶ the level of tolerance displayed to those who view the world from an opposing perspective

▶ the welcoming of views that are challenging

▶ a manner of questioning that is genuinely enquiring and interested

▶ a style of dialogue that emphasises the need to 'seek' rather than the passion to 'tell'.

I have worked with those who have been quick to speak of the necessity to 'bin' people but who have found their own extremes of language tempered by the restraining hand of a generous leader. It is this quality that is the foundation of the 'no-blame' approach.

Generosity is neither kindness nor weakness. It is the action of the open-minded who ascribe importance to enquiry as one of the most subtle but vigorous influencing tools, and who understand the wisdom of a genuine exploration of differing values and points of view before jumping to speedy but poorly judged conclusions. An angry reaction to someone who has let you down may be natural human behaviour. On the other hand, careful scrutiny of the cause of the failure helps the organisation and the people involved to move on, because it contributes to the kind of learning that will eradicate that particular failing another time. It is a million miles from the stormy swagger of the 'macho' manager. Yet it is one of the most mature, exacting, and disciplined of all management behaviours. Soft it is not. But genuine it does need to be. Showing interest in others is an effective way of unearthing the cause of mistakes, of fostering learning, and of lining up your allies. It may seem like a simple device, but it backfires if it is only a show.

The virtue of vigilance

The virtue of vigilance keeps change leaders alert to defensive undercurrents and entrenched baloney that can disrupt, if not wreck, their programme. It involves contact, contact, and more contact. The logistics of such an exercise necessitate a carefully devised system of communication: regular updates, for example, cascade briefings, walkabouts and so on, supported by avid listening on the part of the change leader. But true vigilance cannot end there. Continuous contact also requires 'runners', messengers, or scouts who are out and about daily to offer help, to unravel roadblocks, or to bring in appropriate decision-makers to forge a way through.

Ideally, this scouting is undertaken by those positioned in the hierarchy – supervisors, middle managers, or the front-line staff themselves. But, sadly, all kinds of interferences bring their restraining influence to bear. A member of staff is rebuked for stepping out of line – and never risks an idea again. A supervisor is obliged to communicate via a convoluted hierarchy – and decides it is too bothersome. A middle manager worries about treading on the toes of someone who can adversely affect the chances of promotion. The ambitious regard each other as rivals for honour and glory – and so indulge in the behaviour of concealment and deflection.

Sometimes, therefore, it is circumspect to introduce the 'specials' – dedicated change facilitators and coaches who sit outside the hierarchy and who work in the field every day to act as disentanglers, harmonisers and temperature-checkers. These are the 'galvanisers' of whom I shall say more in the next section.

The virtue of fearlessness

The courage to buck the trend is a special talent. It is one of the qualities of the master risk-taker who possesses the sophistication of judgement and security of instinct that can pick out opportunities for mobilising attitudes or for taking a leap of faith. Soft-skills programmes tend to involve a leap of faith because it is impossible to attribute solely to them any bottom-line benefits, whereas other major changes – a programme of redundancies, for example, or the merging of departments – can be lined up directly against salary savings, cost-effective use of premises, or some other 'hard' measurement.

The fearless leader is not so much the person who vaults into the unknown as the person who is prepared to pursue a course of direction even in the full knowledge of the pain to be endured. When, for generations, machismo has been viewed as admirable, it is painful to jettison it. When technical skills have long been the sole grounds for promotion, a change of emphasis can attract bellicose derision. One of the most remarkable displays of courage is to be found in the most common of all vehicles of expression: our use of language.

The gift of expression

The language of the change leaders is a crucial influencing tool. There is evocative language and provocative language. The former draws people together (for example, organisational or sector jargon, or the style of vocabulary favoured by those united by a profession), the other alienates. Interestingly, provocative language can become evocative language, if there is a lead from the senior team.

When a step-change in culture is required, there is a need to dare to use language on which others may cast aspersions. Not many years ago people who used the feminine as well as the masculine gender in titles (eg chairwoman) were ridiculed. Now it hardly warrants comment. Recently, I was struck by two television interviews in which the director-general of the CBI and the general secretary of the TUC both spoke of the issue of management stress in the workplace. Twenty years ago talk of management stress would have attracted sarcasm or em-barrassment. It was certainly not something to be publicly aired as a concern for the world of work.

Language is integral to the march of progress and is the ally of the change leader who has the nerve not only to use it differently but to keep using it until it is accepted in the culture. In the case snapshot that started this section

Language is integral to the march of progress

(see pages 21–39), I provided an excerpt from an interview with the construction director at the Heathrow Express. I invite you to imagine what it must have been like to be the first person to start using language like 'trust' and 'no blame' in a sector that values the language of the battleground. It is a powerful example of the self-belief and self-possession needed in change leaders, and the tenacity required to hold course despite the ridicule such language may initially attract.

Then look back over the words I took from one of the most senior contractors on the Heathrow Express construction project. Here was a man with a reputation for a tough skin, tough talk, and tough action. Yet he speaks quite unselfconsciously about the value of listening – a soft skill. Consider the impact of this kind of language from this kind of personality.

As a result of the lead and example given by the behaviour of a number of the senior team members, the word 'trust' became regularly used during the construction of the railway, the word 'challenge' was substituted for problem, the term 'no blame' lost its value as a running joke, and the principle of listening moved from sniggering cynicism to acceptance. At one of the team meetings, representatives of management and front line from the project's suppliers, without prompting, produced a statement using the word TRUST as a mnemonic – a fundamental shift in attitude.

Food for thought I

The Heathrow Express change programme was a complex initiative. All parties can learn from it. In these pages I shall own up to what I wish we had done differently:

1   joint action from the senior team on commencement of the programme

2   stronger 'personalising'.

Joint development of the purpose and horizons of change

I have absolutely no doubt that among the most critical factors in sustaining the change programme at Heathrow Express were the vision, determination, and tenacity of the construction director, whose immersion in the programme helped to keep it on course even at its most difficult points, when others might have been tempted to quit. He could, however, have made it less wearing on himself and less risky for the programme.

In our first meetings with senior managers we found that the vision and strategy of the construction director were not always fully apparent or fully understood by many of his colleagues. Indeed, some of them in those early days were bewildered or cynical. One of the principle players in the project confessed to having to talk to others about what exactly the construction director meant by this or that. 'Why doesn't he just say what he wants us to do?', one of them said to me. This was the natural reaction of those who were accustomed to, and valued, the authoritative 'tell' style of conduct and were suspicious of what, on first inspection, seemed to be a move towards shilly-shallying equivocation.

There were very valid reasons at the time for keeping the whole change initiative low key and low profile. The tunnel collapse had seriously dented morale, the HSE was investigating, tension and anxiety were high, and the dynamics of the senior team meant that one-to-one sessions were an appropriate way to introduce the issues of change gradually.

The tunnel collapse had seriously dented morale

Nevertheless, the process would have been greatly eased and accelerated had the senior team *jointly* created the vision at the outset, and committed themselves in front of each other to a standard of behaviour. To reach such a point, given the circumstances and the strong personalities involved, would have required careful and sensitive preparation of the ground (and of individuals) by the construction director and by the change facilitators.

However, that joint stipulation of behaviour and principles, even though private to the senior team and not subject to public broadcast, would have meant that the construction director was not a lone voice in the initial stages of the change programme. It would have been their vision, rather than his vision. It would have set clear expectations and achieved a much clearer understanding in those critical early days. It might also have reduced the need for so much private lobbying-time with individual members of his team, although that investment in personal contact had other valuable benefits in the quality of understanding and the personal relationships we were able to develop, which repaid us dividends later on.

So much reliance on one person had other risks, too. The loss of the key driver would certainly have derailed the process of change. It was not until the arrival of the deputy construction director much later in the project that the 'Prime Mover's' function was partly covered in any sustained or consistent way.

For those of you starting a programme from scratch and with time on your side, it is worth embarking on a process of detailed induction, self-analysis and coaching of individuals, or, if appropriate, of pairs or 'cells' (ie a group of three or four people) in the senior team to forge the mentalities and establish the levels of support that will cover the unexpected or the unforeseen. Putting so many eggs in one basket is not a strategy to be recommended, although we were fortunate to have seen it work on the Heathrow Express project.

Personalising

We chose to limit the 'personalising' phase on this project, persuaded by the criticality of the time-scales and the loose composition of the senior team. It is simpler, of course, to tackle the personalising phase comprehensively when the team has an established track record of working together, and can see itself continuing to function as a unit for some time to come. The Heathrow Express senior management team moved in and out of the project, and was made up not of people from one organisation but from many – a federation of managers from the various contractors and suppliers who had specific responsibilities for different phases of the construction of the railway. Nevertheless, in retrospect, if I faced the same prospect now, I would tackle more fervently the early alignment of the senior team, regardless of their composition or temporary status. I know now that the 'honesty sessions' I describe below (which we called 'time outs' on this project) would have greatly benefited from such an alignment.

While 'time outs' were one of the features of the way people behaved on this project, true 'Honesty in Action Sessions' (HIAs) were not a device we employed, believing them at the time to be too high-risk in a project that had already suffered setbacks. This was a pity. In retrospect, I believe that a team that had achieved so much could have responded well to the discipline as well as the benefits of such an activity. I am sorry not to have tried it with some of the senior teams on the Heathrow Express, although we came close to it with one of the key secretarial groups and (perhaps more significantly, given the potential for real conflict) with the commercial team responsible for the vital activity of managing the project's costs and paying the project's suppliers. The latter was a team made up of people who, on other projects, would have been expected not to trust each other, and indeed would have been specifically tasked to check up, quite deliberately, on each other.

To help you appreciate what I mean by an HIA, here is an example taken from another organisation (although HIAs do not always need to be as structured as this one). As you will see, the level of openness and non-defensiveness lends itself to those teams that have an on-going vested interest in a deep understanding of each other. The longer the association, the more beneficial this kind of contact, and the greater the opportunity to learn from it. This does not preclude short-term projects or temporary teams, however. It means, though, that their starting-point is critical to success, and that their interpersonal skills need already to be at a very high level and the facilitation of such sessions be expertly proficient. Ask yourself what it would take (from yourself and others) to bring your own organisation or your own team to such a point.

Example of an 'HIA'

Barry is the head of a department. His organisation has recently invested in a change programme to move its style away from centralised and hierarchical decision-making, which focused the responsibility for decisions on a few, to one of encouraging decision-making at all levels. He has five managers directly reporting to him who have been used to Barry's fairly tight rein on decisions within the team.

All the managers have a date every month in their diaries for a three-hour joint session with Barry. Their purpose is to recognise good practice, to nip in the bud potential problems, to air issues to prevent what Barry calls 'corridor griping', and to learn from mistakes. The sessions typically begin like this:

Barry Today I think it is Gill's turn to kick off. What would you like to highlight, Gill?

Gill goes through points about various members of the team, including Barry, to identify her perception and experience of her association with each of them over the preceding month. To help her do this, she refers back to a 'recollections' diary in which she has recorded her comments. She is not permitted to make statements without evidence (hence the diary record). Here are some of her comments, which cover compliments and criticisms:

Gill First of all, I would like to thank Jenny for her support earlier this month. I was dealing with a complex disciplinary issue. I don't think it is appropriate to go into details, but I would like to say that the time and the listening ear that Jenny offered made a great deal of difference to how I felt about tackling it.

The second point I would like to make is about a particular incident that highlights the way in which we can, without thinking, undermine each other. One of my staff – Jane Smith – bypassed me to go to Barry (incidentally, Barry knows I'd intended to raise this point because I had already discussed it with him). Without realising it, Barry made a decision which overruled what I had agreed with Jane. I realise there are times when we are all under pressure, but it's the kind of thing that breaks trust. All it required was for you, Barry, to hold off until you had spoken to me. However, you were honest enough to own up to the mistake, and I suppose it is a feature of the newness of the consultative style we have chosen to adopt in place of our old style of referring decisions to Barry. The difficult issue for the two of us now is how we deal with Jane, who has conflicting responses from two managers and, presumably, sees me as being easy to override if she puts her case convincingly enough to Barry. We thought it would be a valuable issue for us to discuss as a team – as a vehicle for examining our own consistency and perhaps agreeing a process for this and other potential areas of confusion so we can make sure that we don't carry on like a team that doesn't know what it's about.

Group discussion follows before Gill continues with her next point.

Each member of the team is invited to make her or his comments. There is no requirement to say something about everyone. Each person sets his or her own agenda. Sometimes, if an issue is important enough, the team agrees to dedicate extra time to it on a separate occasion.

Values exercise

Although we applied a light touch to the personalising phase on the Heathrow Express project, as an alternative to 'Honesty in Action' we did use a vivid 'values exercise' to marshal the values of key members of the senior team.

We used the following process:

▶ values alignment

▶ development of discussion framework

▶ temperature checks

▶ identification of investment points

▶ evolution of support activities.

Figure 4 shows graphically how the process develops.

1 Values alignment

The starting-point for this was the change vision of our sponsor, the construction director, who saw the change programme as delivering one single team rather than the loose federation of separate organisations who were not responsible for those coming after them in the construction process.

Our initial interviews with the construction director generated four important aspects:

▶ his overall purpose

▶ the pressure points as he saw them – and these were our clues to where we should exert our initial support

▶ his definitions and descriptions of the behavioural change he wished to see

▶ the language he wanted to use.

Figure 4
Values Exercise

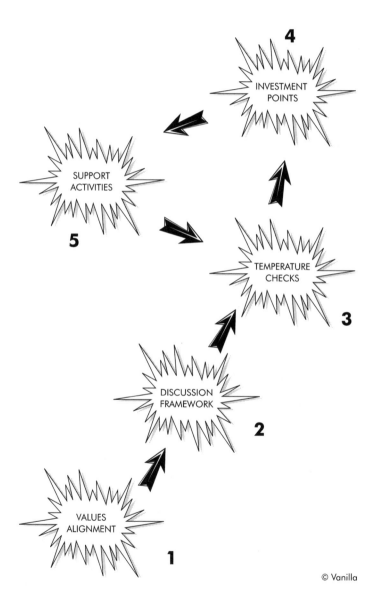

© Vanilla

From this information we devised a series of discussion cards that were used to understand the positions of the other senior team members in relation to the sponsor's vision. We also used this time to identify the people who would be most likely to offer us support and those who were some considerable way from the starting-block.

It is worth noting that some of these interviews were conducted formally and openly, using the cards as the focal point, and others conversationally and unobtrusively without the cards but where the subject of conversation encompassed the issues and values that we had identified. The different approaches were determined by the known style of the managers and by the reactions we anticipated from previous experience.

2 Development of discussion framework

The responses of the senior team were used to develop a simple discussion framework around six points (which came to be known as the 'hexagon' discussions), and we obtained agreement from them on the precise language to be used.

3 Temperature checks

Next, this framework was used as the focus for a series of site-based discussion groups to raise awareness not only of what was meant by the concept of 'single-team working' but also of the behaviours that went with that concept and the issues that would interfere with the acceptance of the new culture.

4 Identification of investment points

The 'hexagon' discussions were a vital temperature check on where people were in relation to the starting-block – and, therefore, what kind of effort and support had to be invested at different locations and with different teams and individuals.

5 Evolution of support activities

Change facilitators, working closely with the change leaders where necessary, used their judgement to develop different activities and types of support to foster change. Regular dialogue with each other built up a system of cross-checks to enable the whole team to draw on the different experiences of each change facilitator.

INTO THE CRACKS

Elusive certainty

A poignantly amusing scene in the musical *Little Shop of Horrors* shows the character Seymour yearning for some direction in his life. Each day he seeks from God an explanation of what he is here for, only to receive the unexpected answer that He is not sure! Seymour has to find the solution from his own resources and self-reliance.

To work comfortably with ambiguity is part of the required disposition of the change facilitator

Case snapshot II

People in organisations are not a mass of humanity. To devise a change programme of 'set pieces' is not only to treat them as though they will all respond in the same way but also to lose sight of your very best opportunity to achieve a fundamental, sustainable step-change in culture – and to do this through a process that is personal and distinctively fitted to the needs of the particular human beings with whom you are working.

This approach to a change programme demands a huge variety of styles from the change facilitators, who will at times find themselves stretching their flexibility and their creativity to the limits in order to make headway. 'Being at work' for a change facilitator entails keeping continuously alert not only to the undercurrents that can sweep away achievements but also to the clues that indicate:

▶ how exactly to tailor an intervention

▶ how precisely to personalise an intervention

▶ how firmly to focus an intervention.

On the Heathrow Express change programme this sometimes resulted in long-term 'coaching' relationships between a change facilitator and others. It also resulted in a number of one-off, specially designed events (such as a communications programme exclusively for those who had to deal with HM Railway Inspectorate). The philosophy underlying this approach was that the investment in 'once only' activities was an appropriate way to recognise the significance to the goal of the construction project of:

▶ individual needs

▶ the variation in individual circumstances

▶ the value of individual contributions.

It is work that can be taxing, yet all-absorbing.

The family way

A short time ago I saw a television interview in which Bob Crandall, chairman and chief executive of American Airlines, spoke most expressively about 'tuning in' to people (although that is not his term but mine). The subject of the interview was the proposed merger between his airline and British Airways, a venture that offered both organisations the challenge of lining up their respective cultures and attitudes. The analogy that

Crandall used was his own marriage of many years in which, as he explained, his wife and he had grown gradually and mutually over the time of their marriage to think very much alike.

The 'family' analogy also proved to be a favourite of the deputy construction director at Heathrow Express. On several occasions I heard him describe the need for the members of the project to demonstrate the tolerance and understanding members of a close family display towards each other. It was one of the accepted tenets of our philosophy as change facilitators, and one that often caused me to reflect on the nature of the constraints (imposed or self-imposed) of the work environment in which, unlike in a healthy home environment, we often find ourselves (or believe we do) – that is, not free to adjust to what suits us.

So, a work set-up may require us to be present daily, even though our personal style means that we are less productive than we would be working from home. Yet we may not feel we can even begin to put this forward to our boss as a regular basis for operating. Or we may believe that it is cheeky to invite a senior manager to discuss an issue over lunch because…well, it isn't done, is it? Or we continue to attend meetings conducted in ways that benefit us little, because to question them is to over step the mark. In a close family we might refuse, or we might ask 'Why?' or suggest 'Why not…?', because that sort of behaviour *is* tolerated.

Small is beautiful

As a team of change facilitators, we were acutely aware of how effective it can be to use small groups to develop 'family' behaviour. We found that we made considerable strides in developing people's attitudes when groups were very small, because that was when people felt more comfortable with questioning and challenging the status quo. We also learned that our flexibility and adjustment to individuals in almost every detail – how we spoke, what we said, what dress code we adopted for this or that situation, where we held training workshops, when we held them, which one of us was allocated to this person or to that activity – deeply affected our ability to make headway in this change programme.

Working with small groups meant in practice that it was more straightforward to:

▶ adapt our own styles to those of individuals

▶ tap in quickly to the mood of a group or an individual

▶ use our judgement to work in whatever way necessary to move forward with that group or individual.

So, to reach people, we would take account of the time to meet them, the location, the size of the group, the best composition of the group, the length of the workshop, and so on.

Some of us conducted meetings or training workshops inside the tunnel itself in order to meet people on their own working territory. Others turned up at 5 am or 11 pm in order to make contact with key people who worked shifts. Any skills training we offered was usually designed carefully around modules of no more than an hour or two. Any case-studies we used were constructed around the real issues we found in the workplace.

The umbrella and the dinosaur

Our engaging of key managers in certain aspects of the programme was such a powerful influencing device that we had to focus their involvement carefully. For example, quite early in the programme we found a need to do something out of the ordinary to shift the attitudes of a group of key middle managers. We refer to this as our 'umbrella and dinosaur' approach, because the rather complex activity we devised for this group, involving the construction director and one of his senior managers as 'moderators' of the attitudes that emerged during the exercise, was based on expressions we had heard people applying to the degree of protection or lack of relevance they believed the new culture of teamwork offered them.

The comfort zone

When we began to work with suppliers, our early contact with some of them indicated that they dreaded the prospect of large seminars at which they would feel out of their comfort zone, and at which they believed they would be pressured to speak against their will. So, we devised for these gatherings a system of mini work groups that allowed people to work in clusters of no more than four or five. The discussion content was tailored to allow them to concentrate on sharply focused elements of the construction process with which they were already comfortable and familiar – resulting in real life in two comfort zones, the larger gathering to accommodate those who obtain a buzz out of being together in a full group, and the informality and fellowship of the 'clusters'.

Tailored support

The depth and duration of our contact with key people on the project meant that we found ourselves in long-term coaching arrangements that proved productive not only for the individuals but also for the influencing of others who were observing, from the periphery, the outcome of personal coaching. We tackled the most difficult personal or interpersonal issues either privately or in advanced team-building sessions that were always carefully designed around the personalities involved and always preceded by 'lobbying' of the key protagonists.

By the time we arrived at the commissioning of the whole railway system, the culture had become sufficiently embedded to allow us to conduct an assessment of the combination of 'soft' skills within the commissioning team. The interventions and internal reputation of another consultant, herself a chartered civil engineer, with whom I worked closely on this assignment, added the insight and credibility of the 'construction' angle to this highly sensitive process.

Change facilitators were there for people from the start of their involvement (introducing them to the 'single-team' philosophy) to the end of their involvement, with an exit programme for those who wished to take stock of their learning on the project.

The latter turned out to be a turning-point for many people. On this project, people had made such an extraordinary journey in many ways that, on the suggestion of one of the project's managers, we devised a series of workshops entitled 'Managing the Future' to encourage people to record and discuss what they had achieved before embarking on the next phase of their careers. We still receive feedback on the value of this workshop from the participants, who had never before stepped back to analyse themselves and their value to a construction project in quite this way.

The exit programme turned out to be a turning-point

To give you a flavour of the different sides of the coaching relationship that was an integral part of our work as change facilitators (consuming probably 70 per cent of our time on the project), and that turned out to be our most powerful influencing mechanism, here are two perspectives: one from a change facilitator who explains the coaching concept and how it was used in practice on the Heathrow Express project, the other from a line manager who drew on her assistance.

The view of the change facilitator

'One of our key roles as change facilitators, and the aspect of our work that consumed the most time, was coaching individuals or small teams. The concept was that coaching would be a vehicle for intensely personal, day-by-day support for different circumstances – for example:

▶ working through a difficult interpersonal issue

▶ putting together an information document

▶ 'trying out' an approach to resolving a point of conflict

▶ practising, in private, a critical presentation

▶ personal analysis and feedback on meetings performance

▶ addressing a specific skills shortfall in private.

It represented, in effect, an investment in personal sounding-boards who helped individuals to *practise*, in a private and risk-free environment, any important aspect of their work – whether a critical interpersonal interaction or an operational process.

The coach was not there to usurp anyone's operational or management responsibilities but to work quietly in the background to help individuals in tackling those responsibilities. The coach would work on developing a person's skill in a specific area, and, in doing so, would help to nurture the kind of attitudes of co-operation and thoughtful behaviour that were the implicit intention of the 'single-team' structure. Even so, despite our best intentions, there was some open hostility from one or two managers who misinterpreted our support as an attempt to show them up. This is where the skills and sensitivity of individual coaches will determine how well you can convert hostility to support.

Most of the effort was unseen except by those directly involved. It was low-profile work. And it was important that recognition went to the managers and the front line, not to the coaches. The change facilitators who took on this coaching role held no hierarchical position in the project, and did not even have a desk or office to call home. This was important: we had to rely on our personal influencing skills, and moved around as we were needed, and so were not attached full-time to any one person or team.

The quality of the relationships we were able to build up was a significant factor not only in our ability to operate but also in contributing to the fact that we were often approached by individuals who needed help. The reputation of individual facilitators tended to grow through word-of-mouth recommendation.

Sometimes a change facilitator would also take a formal training role in order to help with a particular development need. For example, many people were nervous about making presentations at the monthly Suppliers Club. Rather than take them out of the operation for a formal presentation skills course, a change facilitator would coach them, in a short and intensely focused training session, on their specific presentation – supplying feedback on the style of delivery and even the choice of language. The same would often happen with meetings behaviour. For example, when a person's chairing behaviour led to wasted time and effort in meetings, the coach would observe and analyse that behaviour, and together they would work out a better approach to improve the management of future meetings.

One of the most interesting developments was that some coaches became informal communication interfaces – sometimes introducing new members of the project to key contacts, sometimes being approached to act as intermediaries or conveyors of information by those who believed that they lacked the social skills or organisational status to make a particular contact.

So, coaching was essentially about behind-the-scenes support for individuals or very small groups, but the coach might also suggest that a formal training course would be relevant. This was how the supervisory skills training worked – the coach acting as trainer, delivering short workshops on delegation or influencing or motivation, and then working with the course delegates in the field to re-inforce that behaviour and to support the practice and experiment in real life.

'Coaching was essentially behind-the-scenes support'

There were not enough of us to provide everyone – or even every team – with a dedicated coach. So our own judgement on where to focus our efforts was helped by continuous dialogue with the strategists and the site-based managers, with site foremen and with secretarial staff. We had to go to them and make an effort to get to know them. There is no way, I think, this approach would have worked if we had waited for people to come to us. We may of course not always have got the focus quite right in such a complex environment, and it is always the case that any coach will say that he or she would have liked to have done more.

The work could sometimes be very difficult and even disheartening – sometimes it was one step forwards and two back. I think, as a group, we were chosen for our resilience and tenacity as well as for our skills. But when we look around and see the front-liners who have come through to lead induction sessions in the 'single-team' philosophy and culture, and who resolve problems they would previously have passed up to management, or secretaries who lead their own work improvement and training groups, or managers who are reported as being 'changed people from a month ago', or when we receive a telephone call, as I did last week, from someone who has recognised that he needs help on an interpersonal issue (given that emphasis on interpersonal strengths was not even part of his organisation's culture), it is more than just gratifying – it puts you on a real high.'

A line manager from a supplier organisation

'When I joined the project no one talked about "soft skills". At that time, I certainly would not have known what was meant by the term. So, when I was asked to attend a "soft skills analysis session" for managers who were to join the "commissioning team", I really thought it was a waste of time. I was also worried about being judged on skills that, quite frankly, I was not hired to demonstrate. This anxiety was re-inforced when some people were seen to leave the project, and it was rumoured that their management skills rather than their technical skills were the issue.

I didn't know what coaching was. It was never publicised. It was all very low key – and that is one of my criticisms – so we didn't know early enough that this service was available. On the other hand, I can see that maybe if it had been publicised, it would have been ridiculed or rejected. Perhaps its value had to be seen first.

It's like having your own personal listener and observer to test out your behaviour in a risk-free context. The feedback I was given after the soft-skills analysis was both positive and critical – but I just heard the critical. So it was very powerful and, in retrospect, a great privilege to have someone who came to help me through some of the communication and interpersonal issues.

I have never worked this way, and I think some managers would find it too hard to submit to this kind of help and analysis. I'm sure they would see it as loss of face. I was lucky. The coach who worked with me tuned in to my style and my jargon very quickly. I don't think one can underestimate this quality in a coach, just as I don't think one can underestimate the skill and sensitivity it takes to ensure we are not made to feel silly.

It has made me think. The level of detailed feedback has been astounding – for example, analysing even the language I use in meetings, or the way I subconsciously change my style and behaviour when I am with different people. The simplicity of the approach masks the strength of its impact. You never see yourself this way, and when you understand the effect you can have on others, you begin to see why a change in your own behaviour or attitude might be a sensible way to

'I am unrecognisable from the person who used to rant!'

improve your ability to influence other people. I've been told I am unrecognisable in meetings from the person who used to rant! But coaching wasn't available to everyone, so some people would have lost out on the kind of support I had.

I feel that at times in organisations we miss a trick in thinking of communications as vehicles for passing information around. It is as much about enabling this kind of personal unblocking in the workplace, but that probably requires a different approach for workplace com-munications – one that actually holds us to account on what we actually *do* about our own personal standards in dealing with each other. Otherwise we can all get away, can we not, with just nodding in agreement with the principles and saying the right words.

At first I was worried that people would say it was an indictment of my skills that I should need this kind of coaching. Now I look upon it as a refresher course on all those human skills and sides of my personality and character that have been lying in the background for so long, pressured out by the need to operate on a different plane.'

As change facilitators we found gems in unexpected places. These were the people who came forward to help us in the various change activities:

▶ front-line staff who helped to induct newcomers into the cultural aspects of the project, or who resolved a whole range of issues that were a source of irritation to themselves or their colleagues

▶ secretaries who helped us to design and deliver training to their own colleagues and who then went on to develop and run their own continuous improvement groups, not just across the project but beyond it into some of the parent companies

▶ site foremen and supervisors who made presentations about their involvement in the culture

▶ people of all levels who committed themselves to being trained as facilitators to work alongside us.

They all came to be known as 'champions' because of their willingness to champion the change of culture.

I found myself referring to the process as 'sharing silver and gaining gold' – a brilliant exchange, which demonstrated how a personalised approach and individual help and support can uncover a splendid windfall.

8

Gold dust

Putting together a team of change facilitators is a task of considerable consequence, because it is they who are assigned to the substantial responsibility of working day-by-day among the people of an organisation to influence behaviour.

The composition of this key group of influencers rests on a number of qualities. Among the most important are:

▶ personal resourcefulness

▶ each person's threshold of tolerance of uncertainty

▶ the team's process for recharging its batteries.

The value of the intangible

The dilemma of Seymour in *Little Shop of Horrors* that I described at the start of this section reflects the world of ambiguity in which change facilitators have to find a sure footing, relying on personal resourcefulness, a gift for inventiveness and a shrewd capacity to forge productive alliances. How strange that, despite life's lessons on the dilemmas and perplexities of human behaviour, we still seek out those comforting formulae. A recent gathering of change facilitators was reflecting on two of the questions they are most commonly asked by the procurers of their services – 'What model will you be using?' and 'What will the (programme) package look like?' So it is, in these days of the search for the tangible.

As change facilitators, we rely heavily on the intangible – bags of it. The activities of coaching, coaxing and conciliating draw on our:

▶ faith in our judgement

▶ ability to build relationships

▶ enthusiasm

▶ self-motivation

▶ communication skills

▶ innovation

▶ knack for tuning in to different behavioural styles

▶ eye for an opportunity to draw in an ally or convert a doubter.

But to say to customers 'You are buying my judgement' usually causes them a high degree of discomfort. So, some consultants are tempted to offer frameworks and models to quell the disquiet. We have found that it is better to agree with a customer the principles and concepts, and to recognise, from the start, that when we are in the thick of it, instinct, training, experience, common sense, and personal confidence will determine our variety of approach – a long, long way off from formulae.

The galvanisers

Change facilitators are the galvanisers in the field, working tirelessly in the cracks, nooks and crannies in which lurk the obstacles that could stop the show or, just as probably, the hidden supporters who need only a personal approach and a helping hand to emerge. It is work that calls for immense flexibility.

It is, of course, quite natural to want to make it easier on ourselves. But in a curious way, change facilitators who rely heavily on models are actually making life harder for themselves. These are usually the people who, sadly, have lost faith in their own judgement. I have on a few occasions found myself working alongside people who have become so enslaved to models that they cannot break free, even when the writing is on the wall. In difficult change programmes, in which emotions run high and preparedness for the unexpected is part of the armoury of the change facilitator, such people are a constraint on themselves, and so find themselves unhappily losing confidence as soon as their models cease to serve as a protective safety net.

Of all the qualities of effective change facilitators, perhaps the most valuable is the robustness of their personal recharging mechanism. That is because a crusade needs the very best in the front line and, in a change programme, front-line work is not a matter of hierarchy but of activity. Those of you who have worked in the front line of a complex change programme will need little reminding of the effort it takes. The activity of the constant re-inforcement of the desired behaviour, the restoring of dented self-belief, and the renewal of waning interest can be exhausting.

If you are a change facilitator who possesses, in addition to the whole range of qualities listed above, ceaseless energy and boundless self-motivation, you are gold dust, and I hope your sponsors recognise that. It is far more likely, however, that a team of change facilitators will be composed of people with a wide variation of energy levels. Change facilitators owe it to themselves and their sponsors to find ways to keep their batteries recharged. Others feed off you. So it is sensible to keep yourself nourished.

Resilience and integrity – vital assets

As part of your preparation for an extensive change programme, therefore, it is well worth devising a preservation plan for two vital assets that will support you throughout your work – your resilience and your integrity. If you are the leader of a team of change facilitators, then you have a double responsibility, to yourself and to your colleagues.

Fluctuating feelings are a constant feature of the life of a change facilitator. They demand a high threshold of tolerance. Today you may be exhilarated by your success in engaging an ally. Tomorrow you may be seriously shaken by the sharpness of aggression, or by the discovery that someone on whom you had counted for support has revoked his assistance at a crucial juncture. Your own motivation is so important in influencing others that to ignore this 'draining effect' is to risk reducing your influencing capability in the field. Finding your own ways to deflect the dissipation of your enthusiasm, therefore, is not simply desirable. It is quintessential.

There are ways in which you can combat the 'draining effect'. One way is to plan for time away from the project. Another is to distance yourself, if you can, from internal politics. Both of these are easier to achieve when you are hired in as an external facilitator. My team of facilitators worked for over two years on the Heathrow Express project – a long period to retain one's freshness. But the fact that we all worked part-time on the project meant that 'time aways' were built into our operation. Even

Stand back from internal politics

when we were pressed to work full-time, we found methods of working in tandem in order to deliver what was needed, but without losing our recharging mechanism. We believe that our ability to stand back from the internal politics was an outcome not only of our behaviour but also of our part-time association, our lack of hierarchical position, and our lack of an established base or office within the project.

You do not have to be external, however, to devise your strategy. Standing back from the politics demands the personal discipline and judgement to recognise when to keep your own counsel and to understand the ramifications if you do not. Establishing your recharging mechanism requires advance agreement on how your *modus operandi* will accommodate planned 'time away' periods for each member of the team.

Allegiance or responsibility?

This raises another issue. The question of allegiance to your sponsor is not an unusual one. Your integrity in the field depends partly on your reputation for not being seen as the spy of senior management. Given that you have been brought in by senior management, however, the situation has potential for awkwardness. In the end, it is your own behaviour over time and the quality of the relationships you are able to build up that determine whether you are labelled as a player in the game of duplicitous decorum or trusted for your autonomy of mind, freedom of opinion, and independence of judgement.

You may find your sponsors, especially those who lead a lonely life at the helm, drawing increasingly on your partnership. And you may gradually find yourself pulled between allegiance and responsibility. Keep your eye on the prize to retain your sense of proportion. Were you employed to offer your allegiance as a sole adjutant to your sponsor, or to facilitate a successful transition to a new culture? The answer will help you to determine the most appropriate way to operate.

9

Working the wheel

Operating as a coach to individual needs, the change
facilitator will draw on a range of personal skills and assets.

Keeping an open mind about each person is an attribute
to be valued and fostered in a team of change facilitators.
It is:

▶ an aid to helping the different personalities in an
organisation

▶ a pre-requisite for understanding and influencing
work styles and preferences that may be very different
from one's own

▶ a key to developing judgement about the wisest
approach to adopt for this circumstance or that person

▶ (not to be underestimated) a characteristic that
ensures one's own continuous learning.

Buffaloes, bears, eagles, and mice

One of the truly uplifting aspects of the work of the change facilitator is the opportunity, every day, to expose to the light a fresh side of yourself. I call it 'working the wheel'. The Native American's medicine wheel describes the different perceptions and preferences each individual brings to the world. Its proposition is that our responsibility in life is to master not just our own perspective but every other perspective, thereby achieving, by the end of our lives, a completely balanced understanding of humanity. So, the 'wheel' defines the buffalo's approach as analytical and logical, the bear as valuing relationships, the eagle as hovering above the detail, seeing clearly the connections and patterns in data and making rapid sense of arguments, and the mouse as enjoying detail and conducting itself right in among the minutiae of life.

The medicine wheel adds the dimensions of colour and direction to these symbols, thereby acknowledging the complexity of human behaviour and personality – for example, you may be a green eagle, looking outwards. Working your way around the wheel from your own starting-point to become an expert in all the different perspectives is said to be the goal of life.

As change facilitators, we have the privileged chance to work the wheel because we are right in among all the different perspectives every day, and the soundest way to influence is to step over to the other person's side. It calls for heightened observation, as well as the ability to adjust your own style to another's (for example, altering your language, or finding a way to demonstrate your acceptance of values that may be different from your own). The prospect of testing your own flexibility in this way is a stimulating one, offering an inducement to personal growth as well as an expedient route to influencing.

Recognising the rainbow

Apart from your adaptability, you will also find yourself testing your judgement in all kinds of ways: how to draw in your allies (indeed where to find your most likely allies), when to confront the mischievous, what kind of coaching approach to utilise, and so on.

Did you know that each one of us sees a rainbow differently and uniquely because of the way sunlight bounces around each raindrop? Practised change facilitators tend to be adept at finding their own personal rainbows around the patch. Different facilitators will have different allies. And sometimes you will find your allies in places where others tell you there is only barren soil,

Each one of us sees a rainbow differently

because they have viewed the situation from their own angle, which may be very different from yours. This is one of the advantages of working as an external facilitator, because you will usually arrive without preconceptions about individuals and be inclined to take people on their contribution at the time, not on their history in the organisation.

The porcelain egg

I once worked alongside a salesforce that used the term 'porcelain egg' to denote a sales prospect who, no matter how hard they tried, never bought. The tendency, however, was for the entire team to write off a porcelain egg because of one person's experience, failing to appreciate that one salesperson's porcelain egg may be another's fruitful encounter.

There are no porcelain eggs for the team of change facilitators that deploys its resources in wise and close co-ordination to accommodate the whole range of styles that make up any collection of human beings.

The skill is to match the style of the coach with the style and need of the recipients. Some coaches will possess the boldness to operate at one level, others will use their tenacity in chipping away at another. Some may be best in the vanguard, making first contact, putting out feelers and setting the scene, before passing the baton to those who will develop long-term relationships.

There are endless ways to capitalise on the array of qualities in a team of change facilitators, but the driving force should be 'try, try and try again', even in the face of those who insist that such-and-such will never succeed. The secret is to work in the spirit, perhaps (if it is not too inflated a notion), of Sir Barnes Wallis, inventor of the bouncing bomb, who, in response to those who believed his vision too fanciful, remarked that there was no greater thrill in life than first proving something was not impossible and then showing how it could be done. I have seen people whom colleagues have rudely written off as 'fossils' emerge from a thoughtfully aligned coaching relationship with fresh vigour and previously untapped talent.

Crusty and cracker

Just as there are no porcelain eggs, so there are no 'crusties' in the mentality of those who work as a coach in the field. I remember undertaking an interesting assignment with a team of extraordinary extroverts who branded as 'crusties' (crustaceans) those who had the temerity to decline their rowdy social gatherings, preferring more reflective pastimes. The 'crusties' were compared unfavourably with the 'crackers', whose wit and spark positively 'cracked' the air.

'Introvert' is not a dirty word, however. Big seminars and flourishing public occasions tend to favour the preferences of the extrovert. Field coaching is perhaps the most impressive, yet prudent, way to reach out as an influencer in a change programme to all the different styles and needs around you. It allows the change facilitator to:

▶ personalise attention

▶ analyse and offer feedback on soft skills in a discreet but personally powerful way

▶ tailor support to those who do not respond to large gatherings.

It also offers opportunities, in private, to challenge the mischievous or to tackle destructive attitudes. The latter is more common a requirement than you may think. Even some of the most senior people will often refrain from raising an objection in a meeting and, the moment they depart, will huddle with another like-minded person to declare that the agreements of the meeting are doomed to failure. When the meetings have been critical (such as the scouting meetings on the Heathrow Express project, which were designed to flag up potential show-stoppers), such behaviour is unhelpful, and it deserves a positive challenge – the kind of challenge that can be made by a coach behind the scenes, if necessary, to encourage a more constructive participation next time around.

There is, therefore, a high level of detail implied in a coaching relationship. If you remember that the change facilitator in a soft-skills programme is coaching not the technical but the personal, you will obtain a strong perception of just how sensitive a skill this is. The case snapshot attached to this section offered the impressions of a line manager who was part of just such a coaching arrangement, and it demonstrates the importance, in practice, of this type of relationship.

10

Thinking triggers

The nature of interpersonal coaching in the field, supplying as it does the kind of intensely personal support that allows individuals to tap into a source of help for the development of their skills or the resolution of a difficult communication issue, creates its own potentially ticklish consequences of supply and demand.

It is sensible and far-sighted to establish a network of allies around the organisation to introduce an added dimension to the support you offer and to help maintain the impetus of change.

Locating your allies

The nature and activity of coaching ensure that change facilitators work in a real-life laboratory. This can be so interesting and inspiring that you may find yourself taking on too much. In a lengthy or sizeable operation, the sheer scale of the task means it is sensible for the efforts of the coach to be artfully focused, and this can entail working *through* others who serve as your *in situ* allies. These are your tendrils who enable you to keep in touch with developments, work alongside you at times, and help you to select the areas that will repay your investment.

Some of your allies will identify themselves, coming forward of their own accord to offer their assistance as co-facilitators or to act as points of contact for the dissemination of information. Others may need some enticement. The clues will be there for your observation and response. From formal discussion groups or informal conversations you will find yourself gathering evidence of individual attitudes that will help you to pin-point your allies.

Listen out for the clues in the language. To help you, Figure 5 (on page 120) provides an example of the differences between 'rich thinking' and 'restricted thinking'. The rich thinkers are your natural helpmates, but even the restricted thinkers can, with coaching, become solid supporters if you (or a colleague) invest in the relationship.

Remember also that restricted thinkers can serve as a useful feasibility-check, pointing out the pitfalls that others may not, in their enthusiasm, recognise. But when speed and pace are an issue, such people are not obvious material for your early, crucial efforts. They need more time, and this is best spent after you have set up some initial, successful alliances.

Rich thinkers can be located at all levels of an organisation. Some of the most promising allies (and influencers) are to be found among secretarial and support staff. I am astonished how often they are overlooked. In one professional organisation, I was told that a particular training programme was inappropriate for the 150 secretaries because they were not the fee-earners – this in spite of the fact that, in taking on some of the administrative

Figure 5

Natural and Potential Allies

Rich thinkers	Restricted thinkers
Talk of investments, benefits, value	Talk of costs
Have their eye on the prize at the end (eg the goal of the project/ their own career goals)	See mainly the constraints and boundaries of the immediate moment
Tend to ask 'How?'	Tend to ask 'Why?'
Vividly see the possibilities and potential (offer ideas)	Fear the penalties and reprimands (offer excuses)
Look around and think ahead (seek active involvement)	Look down and away (recoil from involvement)
Adopt the resolver's philosophy – 'Look and you may not see, think and you may not see, but the two together will resolve the issue'	Adopt the relegator's philosophy – 'Look to another, think why not'

© Vanilla

work previously undertaken by the so-called fee-earners (who were thereby freed for other revenue-earning activities), they were positively affecting the bottom line.

Your allies may need special training or coaching in order to be effective in the field. For example, you may find that they:

▶ will play a part in the cultural induction of newcomers, for which they may need help with their presentation or communication style

▶ may prove to be valuable assistants in team-building activities, for which they will need to be most carefully briefed on the timing and nature of their participation.

The thoughtful development and training of your allies is a valuable activity that will reward you many times over.

Part of the sense of achievement you acquire as a change facilitator is in transferring your expertise to others, leaving a valuable trail of re-inforcers wherever you operate. This is sound strategy. The successful transition from one culture to another is greatly strengthened by the sharing of craft, recognition, and goodwill. It also frees the change facilitator to move on to other areas that need attention, thereby progressing the culture to pastures new and recharging themselves in the process.

11

Working with the grain

The significance of tuning in

Choice of *activity* in a change programme is an outcome of personal judgement, appropriateness of timing and, above all, the nature of relationships.

The ability to build relationships is so fundamental a requirement for change facilitators that it will take precedence over all the other attributes and qualities on which they will find themselves drawing.

Weighing up behaviour

One of the greatest tests of the versatility and judgement of the change facilitators lies in the variety and innovation of their approaches to fitting in with the needs and preferences of an organsiation's people. You will often hear change facilitators talk about 'tuning in' to a situation. What they mean by this is that the weighing-up of individual or team behaviour, in this situation or that, determines the nature of the activities they select for use – for example, deciding:

▶ which level of facilitation to employ

▶ whether to draw in senior managers (and which one)

▶ whether to avoid dealing with a particular team as a group because they show signs they will respond better to one-to-one coaching

▶ whether a discussion of a case-study will move people on from a block

▶ what kind of case-study to design.

These are not a matter of applying a model but of applying one's own sharp intuition and plain good sense to a normal, human situation.

Disentangling, advocating, and moderating

Whenever they need to manage meetings formally, the change facilitators, with their ear to the ground and a feel for the mood of the moment, can steer the style of the meeting through their own choice of behaviour. Three separate levels of facilitation can be selected. In the first, the change facilitator acts as a disentangler, in the second as an advocate, and in the third as a moderator. The choice of approach is linked to the purpose of the intervention, as well as to the attitudes of those involved.

The disentangler

The 'disentangler' takes care of the process of a discussion, freeing participants to focus on the content and ensuring that no one person dominates proceedings. The disentangler role is also used less formally – for example, in introducing individuals to others in the organisation with whom they might usefully team up. On the Heathrow Express project we found ourselves making heavy use of this particular activity to help shy colleagues or to forge a way for productive relationships outside the established hierarchy.

The advocate

The 'advocate' is the change facilitator in an influencing role – guiding a situation to a point at which a team may need to arrive before you can move the programme on. The achievement of the goal may demand a considerable amount of lobbying and research. For instance, you may find yourself working hard to convince a senior manager of the need to attend a much-needed question-and-answer session with the front line for which there is no warning of the questions. If this is not his or her preferred style, resistance may be high.

The moderator

The last role – that of the 'moderator' – is the most time-consuming in its preparation. I tend to use it in those circumstances that would otherwise result in an impasse, in order to jolt attitudes out of the mire. It requires a high degree of preparation and the devising of a detailed case-study based on actual events and attitudes you have found in the workplace – meaningful to the group, therefore, but sufficiently disguised not to expose individuals. It uses a wider range of skills than either of the other facilitative styles. You may find yourself:

▶ encouraging the unaccustomed airing of feelings in the group

▶ testing the basis for derogatory views held about an individual

▶ searching out ways to help a group control the excessive influence of one person, or helping to restore the goodwill of a team in disarray after a badly managed 'honesty session'.

It is a style to be used after careful reflection and with careful management.

Part of the lining-up of skills in the team of change facilitators involves deciding who is best suited to each of these roles, because they draw on different scales of influencing ability and preparation.

Deductions and decisions

Working with the grain includes working with an individual's style, language, and preferred activity. It is the quickest way to carry people with you in a change programme. But it does require a readiness to discard your best-laid plans, your models, or your carefully structured cases and to change course if you find a planned activity is not working for the group you are with at the time – which is one of the reasons that I earlier emphasised the limited value of a programme of pre-ordained activities.

In determining what is an appropriate activity, as I have tried to demonstrate in case snapshot II, there is no substitute for the personal judgement of a change facilitator and for good relationships between the change facilitator and those he or she is seeking to influence. It is sad to see people suppress their own, perfectly sound judgement in favour of set frameworks, even when they are not the best tools for the circumstance.

The appropriateness of timing adds another dimension to that choice. The case snapshot illustrates how, by the time the team to commission the whole system operating the Heathrow Express railway was established, the culture had moved on far enough to allow us formally to analyse the 'soft' skills of key team members. By then people had grown accustomed to the emphasis on 'soft' skills. Nevertheless, we took care to speak to as many people as possible before the assessment. The lobbying of those who expected to join the commissioning team served three important purposes:

▶ It prepared people for what was to come.

▶ It provided the material (real attitudes and issues) that formed the basis of the exercises used in the formal process of team and individual analysis.

▶ It established professional contact and a helpful, professional relationship with people who would be receiving personal feedback from us after the exercise.

Sound relationships, sound results

The relationships that change facilitators build with others are absolutely fundamental to their ability to operate. What begins, say, as 'lobbying' time can quickly become 'relationship' time, and the development of good relationships is what determines the success of many of the activities you could choose to undertake on a change programme. On one level, a good relationship with a change leader determines the depth of that person's involvement alongside a change facilitator. For example, I have used senior managers in a trouble-shooter role on workshops carefully devised to suit the style of those managers.

On a more personal level, the kind of one-to-one coaching relationship I described in the case snapshot is only workable if good relations have been established. Relationships affect the acceptability of a coaching arrangement. And acceptability is the route to 'stickability' and the sustainability of a programme of change. Don't skimp on this particular investment! The ability to build good relationships is a key quality in a change facilitator. Think carefully about its significance when putting together your team of change facilitators.

Working with the grain includes the recognition of where your sources of 'real' (as opposed to 'official') information lie.

Successful change facilitators work with real information, so as not to squander their opportunities. Front-line staff are among

Front-line staff are valuable sources of real knowledge

the most valuable sources of real knowledge. Supervisors, secretaries, and all those operators who are immersed in the day-to-day detail of a process know how things *really* work, as opposed to how they are meant to work. This makes them not just a powerful source of information but a source of wisdom that can be applied to the improvement of the operation. The change facilitators who tap this source usually find diamonds, even among the ruts and the resistance. And a little care and attention can convert them into the cutting-edge of a change programme.

As we saw in the case snapshot, at Heathrow Express these were the people who came to be known as 'champions', because they came forward to champion different aspects of the change programme. Working closely with individual change facilitators with whom they had built solid relationships, they worked behind the scenes to influence their own colleagues, and part of their influencing style was to resolve the issues they knew were the source of irritation in the front line. Some of these were hygiene issues connected with the food or rest facilities available, others were about the disentangling of communication blocks. Some of the champions went further and worked as co-facilitators in inducting newcomers to the 'single-team' philosophy.

The Chinese lantern...and a final thought on behavioural flexibility

One element of a flexible change programme is the degree to which the whole company of activist roles (Prime Movers, Dedicated Ambassadors, Galvanisers) can be moulded and mobilised to any circumstance. I like to think of this unofficial structure (a *behavioural*, not an organisational one) as a versatile one that unfolds to meet different circumstances, like a folding Chinese lantern (see Figure 6, page 130) that can shrink to a flat arrangement in which the segments are indistinguishable but can also expand to full size when needed. There is no hierarchical top or bottom to the lantern: people's behaviour unfurls and reveals the backing of a person's status only as needed.

The unfolding of events in a change programme demands no less a degree of flexibility from its key protagonists. So, although at major seminars it may be desirable to be able to differentiate the decision-makers in the hierarchy, at certain team-building sessions the encouragement of openness and the advancement of learning may depend on the levelling out of position. This is not achieved by artificial pronouncements but by the *behaviour* of those involved.

Figure 6

Versatile Structure: the Chinese Lantern

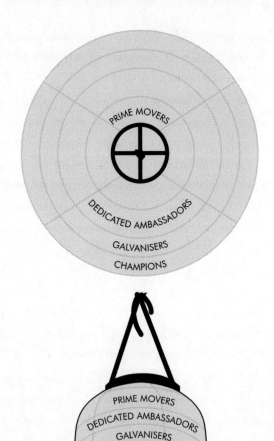

© Vanilla

Food for thought II

I have a final challenge for all those who achieved so much cultural change in the construction of the Heathrow Express railway.

There were some who said 'rubbish'. There were many who said 'Too difficult', 'Too pie-in-the-sky', or expressed their reactions in far more colourful and unmistakable language. There were people who rejected – and even some who, sadly, undermined – the efforts of others.

Despite all this, there were those of you who hung in there and made personal leaps and cultural strides. What extraordinary achievements and efficiencies could your organisations or your next projects reach if, with your participation as change influencers, *everyone* contributed as you did?

TAKE-AWAY TIPS

Take-away tips for change leaders

Line up the mastery of the culture at the top

The senior team (board members, directors, heads of function, project leaders) are the most powerful role models in a programme of change. Their own behaviour is fundamental to the success of a change programme. So begin with a strong investment in the behaviour of the most senior managers.

They could use the following five-stage approach to analysing and agreeing on the behavioural standards that they, as the change leaders who have initiated a change programme, would be expected to demonstrate to the rest of the organisation:

1   **Start by examining, privately, our own attitudes and behaviour, using the TL^2 framework in Chapter 5.**

2. **Use an independent change facilitator, in the role of coach, to talk through the responses, to discuss the gaps, and, most importantly, to agree a plan for handling the gaps in the individual styles within the team – for example, by pairing off with another team member with different attributes, or by working privately with the coach to address the shortfall.**

3 **From each of these independent sessions generate:**

i   draft standards of conduct for the senior team

ii   practical examples to illustrate that conduct

iii   a system for monitoring, re-inforcing, or correcting that conduct.

4 **Get the senior team together to discuss and agree the behavioural standards.**

5 Use these standards for regular temperature-checks and adjustments as the programme unfolds. Depending on how far advanced our own interpersonal skills are, these temperature-checks can be conducted privately, undertaken in the chosen pairs or cells, or, as an advanced team-building session, facilitated independently.

Take-away tips for change facilitators

▶ Take the trouble really to explore the value and goals of the change sponsor(s).

▶ If they are people who have not been involved in anything like this before, take the time to provide practical illustrations of the kind of involvement you will be inviting them to undertake.

▶ Encourage the 'personalising' of the desired change (see Chapter 5).

▶ Understand what the back-up organisation is (see Chapter 6 on the roles of the Prime Movers and Dedicated Ambassadors): there may be critical occasions on which you will need the support of key people. Who will be their substitutes?

▶ Having understood with whom and what you are dealing, take stock of the strengths of your own team. Have a broad (but flexible) framework for whom you would use for different phases or activities in the programme.

▶ Your personal motivation is absolutely critical to your success as a change facilitator. You cannot afford to become stale. Be clear and honest about your personal boundaries: if you allow yourself to be influenced into a position with which you are uncomfortable, you will let down the rest of your team. Take account of how much and what kind of involvement will ensure that you are truly motivated.

During the programme

▶ Use the vision of the senior team as the basis for your first discussion groups or temperature-checks within the organisation.

▶ Use carefully chosen pilot groups or personal lobbying of key people to test out your choice of language for these meetings.

▶ In every meeting or interaction, take note of the positive attitudes that can be used to support you – your allies in the field.

▶ Be ready to discard your plans if a group or individual is not responding.

▶ Invest in personal relationships – through one-to-one coaching of key people, or through introducing individuals to helpful contacts in other parts of the project or organisation.

▶ Use your judgement to invest in variety – people are different. Tap into that.

▶ However resilient you believe yourself to be, it is wise to take some time away from the assignment, especially if it is a lengthy one, to keep yourself fresh. You may not notice the reduction in your energy. Others will.

▶ Work in tandem with another facilitator, if necessary – for example, to handle a particularly thorny issue.

▶ Use each other – to bounce ideas around, to check details, to unburden the stresses and strains you will inevitably experience (but do keep this private to the team of change facilitators).

Post-programme take-away tips for everyone who has learned from the experience

▶ Take stock of your own learning, privately or together, depending on your style and preference. Change programmes are always abundant with uncommon opportunities for your personal growth. Which have benefited you? If you have involved yourself to any substantial degree, you will almost certainly find you have made huge strides in your own development as a professional and as a person, which will determine the nature of your contribution another time.

▶ If you can, keep in touch with your best allies. The nature of organisational life will throw up opportunities in the future for you to learn from their experiences.

Index